It's O.K.
to Be a
Woman Again

ELIZABETH SKOGLUND

It's O.K.
to Be a
Woman Again

Fleming H. Revell
Old Tappan, New Jersey

Unless otherwise identified, Scripture quotations are from the King James Version of the Bible.

Verses marked TLB are taken from *The Living Bible,* copyright © 1971 by Tyndale House Publishers, Wheaton, Ill. Used by permission.

Scripture quotations identified AMPLIFIED are from the Amplified New Testament © The Lockman Foundation 1954–1958, and are used by permission.

Scripture quotations identified PHILLIPS are from THE NEW TESTAMENT IN MODERN ENGLISH, Revised Edition—J. B. Phillips, translator. © J. B. Phillips 1958, 1960, 1972. Used by permission of Macmillan Publishing Co., Inc.

Scripture quotations identified WEYMOUTH are from WEYMOUTH'S NEW TESTAMENT IN MODERN SPEECH by Richard Francis Weymouth. Published by special arrangement with James Clarke & Company, Ltd., and reprinted by permission of Harper & Row, Publishers, Inc.

Skoglund, Elizabeth.
  It's OK to be a woman again/Elizabeth R. Skoglund.
    p.   cm.
  ISBN 0-8007-1597-7
  1. Women—United States—Attitudes.   2. Women's rights—United States.   3. Women's rights—Religious aspects—Christianity.
4. Femininity (Psychology)   I. Title.
HQ1426.S55 1988
305.4′2—dc19   88-11497
                                                             CIP

Copyright © 1988 by Elizabeth R. Skoglund
Published by the Fleming H. Revell Company
Old Tappan, New Jersey 07675
Printed in the United States of America

To my mother,
Elisabeth Alvera Benson Skoglund,
who did not automatically play the role
of the stereotypical woman of her time
but rather chose and fulfilled
her own unique, God-directed role as woman.

CONTENTS

SIX

SEVEN

EIGHT

INTRODUCTION

Women once again want to be women. For centuries woman's history has been checkered with extremes and frustrated by radical changes. Woman has ruled, and she has been enslaved. She has been worshiped and despised. In order to have equality, at times she has given up her distinctive role as woman. But then to be woman she has often relinquished her equality. Only rarely has she been respected with equality of treatment, yet been allowed to fulfill her unique God-given role as woman. Perhaps at no other time in woman's history has she enjoyed the opportunity for both equality and uniqueness that she has today.

As a counselor who spends a good deal of her time dealing with women and their confusion over "who is woman?" I see many women who do not feel that it is a good time to be a woman at all. They want equal rights, but they also want men to treat them as women; and they don't realize that they can have both! They confuse having worth with becoming a cheap imitation of man. In essence, they go to extremes to avoid extremes.

For some the long-range benefits of equal rights have hardly seemed worth it. Woman has put on her pin-striped suit and business tie, only to come home and find that her children have been neglected by the baby-sitter, while her husband has left her for someone else who doesn't mind being a woman and treating him like a man.

For in the confusion, men's roles become unclear also. Some women wonder why their husbands have become docile and ineffective, when that was all they could become, if they were to survive the onslaught of domination inflicted on them by their overaggressive wives who are afraid of losing their rights. The assignment of domestic roles, like single parent and primary homemaker, has further diminished in some men whatever male ego has survived in a society that has suddenly decided that it's OK for Dad to be a housewife, yet has failed to prepare him for that task.

In contrast to the confusion, however, and perhaps in part because of the growth that has occurred during the confusion, a new-old woman is emerging in the world today. She is a new woman because we have not seen her as a model for women in general for a long time. She is an old woman because she has always existed. She is Deborah as she leads Israel to war in the Old Testament. She is Golda Meir leading the Jews back to Israel after World War II. She is Amy Carmichael saving children in the south of India. She is Mrs. Douglas MacArthur supporting her famous general-husband during World War II. She is the liberated woman of biblical history. She is a multitude of women throughout all of time.

Today's new-old woman has potential for growth, opportunity for equality, and a choice in roles. She can compete with pride in the marketplace, and she can with equal dignity stay at home and raise children. Or she can do both, although perhaps not always at the same time! Above all she can still be woman, no matter what her role. She can make a cup of coffee for man, and he can open the door for her without either of them damaging their roles. She can be woman without sacrificing her equality, and he can therefore be man once again.

As a child I had the blessing of having parents who both took great pains to raise me with a wide scope of choices for my life. Being a woman was never considered a liability. Just two months before my mother's sudden death, I wrote in her copy of a book I had just published:

> With gratitude for all the years of believing in my dreams
> and for the help in making them come true.

If my father had still been alive, it would have been inscribed in both their books. For while they didn't push me into the formation of my role in life, they did support me. And they made me believe that the options were endless.

As I grew up, focusing on the will of God became the rudder of my life, directing me in the course God had planned for me from before my birth. The result has been a life that sometimes is right on course for women of my time, but as often as not has taken a turn that is not the average direction for a woman. I had a career when it was popular for women to get married and stay at home. I also have had that career when it has been the "in" thing to do.

Because I didn't have to keep changing my concept of women's roles, I have always had a singular focus that has kept me from the vacillation I so often see in the women

whom I counsel. My direction has changed at times, sometimes drastically, and new goals have presented themselves. But the changes have been the result of decisive
thinking and divine guidance, rather than the random outcome of a new popular fad dictating an alternate trend for
woman.

In our view of the new-old woman today, we have come
full circle to the point where it's truly OK to be a woman
again, in the best definition of the word. We can enjoy our
uniqueness without losing our opportunity. We can embrace the responsibilities without denigration. We can be
feminine without losing our sense of worth.

It's OK to Be a Woman Again is a positive book that
celebrates the woman within each of us. It is about women,
but I have written both to women about themselves and
each other and to the men who deal with them. This is not
just another book on women. It does not fight the cause of
woman's liberation, yet it gratefully accepts some of the
positive results of certain women's-rights activities and
does not admonish woman to roll back time, so to speak,
and ignore her God-given rights. This liberating book does
not pretend that women are not women or deny our femininity. Instead it extols it, shows where woman has
emerged from, what she has gone through in the process,
and where she has ended up. I will talk about roles and
worth, careers and relationships, and old-fashioned femininity. We'll look at sex and childbearing. *It's OK to Be a
Woman Again* tells what the new-old woman has become
and how she has done it.

It's O.K.
to Be a
Woman Again

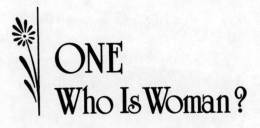

ONE
Who Is Woman?

It was Saturday, December 6, 1941. The year 1941 had been the year of our family's big move from Chicago to southern California. For my parents, eleven-year-old sister, and me it had been a year of great personal change. With Christmas and the end of the year approaching, added to the formation of plans for my father's return from his temporary defense work in Seattle, life appeared to be once again settling down for us as a family. The world around us was at war, but our own personal world as a family felt secure and safe. The war, after all, was "over there."

For me Saturday the sixth was much like any other Saturday. I awakened slowly to the aroma of my mother's Swedish coffee cake baking in the oven. For most of the day my mother cleaned house and washed clothes in the old washing machine, which ended its course by feeding wet clothes through a wringer and then turning them into boardlike, semidried strips that were ready to be hung out to dry on the outside clothesline. As a three-year-old full of curiosity I eagerly watched this process for a while; but at last, bored with my observation of household tasks and a little young to be of any practical help, I spent a major portion of the rest of the day playing tea party with my cat Fluffy and my friend from up the street.

Dinner came early, and the preparations for the night and for Sunday's activities began. My major task was to cooperate with my mother in washing my long hair and setting it in big, bulky metal curlers. Such a process was a necessary prerequisite for wearing curls rather than braids to Sunday school the next day. Still it made Saturday night sleep somewhat more fitful than that of any other night in the week.

Yet on this particular Saturday night as the household settled down to sleep, something out of the ordinary kept my mother awake. My aunt Ruth had recently returned from missionary work with the China Inland Mission in the north of China, and still tired, she fell into an early, deep sleep in the front bedroom, which we used as a sewing room when she wasn't there. My sister, and even I in spite of my curlers, quickly fell asleep in the room we shared. All seemed well; the house was soon quiet. Yet in her room my mother felt no such peace. As her uneasiness mounted she got out of bed and began to pace the floor and pray. Soon she was on her knees praying, increasingly wondering if my father was all right. She did not know exactly what she was supposed to pray about, but with a deepening sense of awareness, she knew that something was terribly wrong.

Such an experience had only happened to her once, years before, when she and her mother had spent anxious days in prayer that had focused itself on my aunt Ruth, who was at that time in China. Then, too, there had been that deepening sense of something wrong. Months later, by mail that came slowly by boat in those days, my mother and grandmother discovered that during their period of concern and prayer a Chinese doctor deep in the interior regions of China had despaired of my aunt's life as she lay near death from typhus fever. Miraculously, she had lived, and at the same time the burden for prayer thousands of miles away had lifted.

On this Saturday night in December, my mother felt that same burden to pray. But this time the focus was even less clear. She could only pray in the dark, so to speak, and trust that God, who knew all, would use those prayers where they were needed. Early in the morning on Sunday, December 7, 1941, she turned on the radio and found out that Pearl Harbor had been bombed by Japan. Within a short time the United States was also formally at war with Germany and Italy. The war that had been "over there" moved a little closer.

I will not know until eternity the specific impact of my mother's prayers on that December night almost a half a century ago, but I do know that some very deep sensitivity to the leading of the Holy Spirit caused my mother to pray through the night on that historic weekend. It was not just chance. I was only a child at the time, but I realized with awe that my mother walked with God. The idea that the ultimate definition of the ideal woman could not exist apart from the concept of godliness was deeply imprinted upon my mind.

In those early years, to me, my mother was the embodiment of woman. She cooked delicious meals, kept house, nurtured her children with stories and biblical teaching, and she supported my father in his work with her practical help as well as with her deep belief in him, which so visibly encouraged him. But she had other sides to her, too. At one time she had been a buyer in antiques for a major department store in Chicago. Throughout her life she was a professional artist who won awards in competition with many prominent male artists, at times including my father, who was also an artist. They competed, but more often than not my parents were mutually supportive in their artistic endeavors. Fortunately, too, they both specialized in slightly different areas of art, so the times of direct competition were relatively few.

On that weekend in 1941, however, in a new way my mother had shown that she had an independent walk with God, which was the basis of all of her life decisions. Early in life I learned from her that to be woman was to be someone very special in God's Kingdom.

Who is woman? The role cannot be stereotyped into one easy definition. Nor can we restrict it by prejudice. The specific definition is fluid and flexible. Yet to be a woman is to be someone very distinct from being a man. Indeed, to be a woman is to be totally opposite of some cheap imitation of a man. For the difference between a man and a woman extends far beyond separate reproductive functions or the contrast exacted by mere cultural conditioning. For incorporated into the obvious overall intent of God Almighty not to make men and women the same, from just a biochemical perspective, there are vast internal differences that forever make it impossible for a woman to be like a man either physically or temperamentally.

Not long ago a woman deep into the cause of women's

rights came into my counseling office after the death of her eight-year-old son. The question she asked repeatedly was: "My husband has been deeply crushed by Johnny's death. But at least he can go on living. I almost can't. What's wrong with me? Why is it hitting me harder? I was the one who thought that I didn't even need children to make me happy. But now I find myself with a deep maternal void that I never knew existed. I hurt as I never thought I could."

There were several answers to her question. But in my mind I couldn't help remembering something another woman had told me a few months earlier. She had been counseling with her physician after the death of her baby. At one point the doctor had said: "If a man sees his wife and child fall over a cliff, he will reach first for his wife. If a woman sees her husband and child fall over the same cliff, she will reach for her child first." Simplistic? Perhaps. But there is truth in this illustration, which graphically points out just one facet in the many differences that exist between men and women.

At times, I feel, we women fear admitting that we are truly different from men, because we feel that somehow that implies inferiority. We are afraid we will lose our rights. It is not strange that we should feel that way, since there was a time in this country when women could neither own property nor vote. If a woman's husband lived in chronic infidelity, for example, a woman had to suffer in silence, for without her husband, she possessed nothing. She could not afford freedom! The injustices toward woman have been great, and some of them still exist. However, equality with men has nothing to do with being like a man. We are marvelously different, but completely equal in value. We are different in kind, but equal in worth. We can have our rights and still be women. To deny that has been a major injustice thrust upon us by some of those who have fought for women's rights. Yet in all fairness to them, let us never forget that as a result, in part, of some of the activities of these women's-rights groups, many women today enjoy such benefits as equal pay for equal work.

Just as the solution to the problems of equality does not lie in trying to become a cheap imitation of a man, so the roles of a woman cannot be easily defined by saying, at the one extreme, that all women should stay at home or, at the other, that all women should be in the marketplace. The roles of women are as varied as they are for men, perhaps more so; and those roles may change many times, even within the life cycle of any one woman.

In addition to the tremendously positive role models I had in my mother and in her sisters, my aunts, certain more public women like Anne Morrow Lindbergh and Catherine Marshall have also been examples to me of ideal women. Both were thoroughly feminine, yet they were successful in careers that could have been the envy of any man. Throughout their lives, however, each played many roles at different times. They did not try to play all the roles at any one time. They didn't try to do it all!

By the time Catherine Marshall married again, following the death of her first husband, Peter Marshall, she was a successful writer in her own right. Yet confronted with a new husband and fairly young children to raise, she temporarily gave up her priority of writing. Later she returned to that career and continued in it until her death, at the end of writing the book *Julie*. Throughout her life she played several roles, ranging from the domestic one of wife and mother at home to the more public one of author.

In the same way Anne Morrow Lindbergh had periods in which she was primarily the mother of her children. Then there were intervals of time where she not only accompanied her famous aviator husband on some of his very risky yet historic flights, but she herself actually learned to fly. Somewhere always woven in among these other roles was again the role of author.

For some women the roles may not change that much throughout their lifetimes. They may prefer to make homemaking a lifelong commitment, with other minor roles in the arts or even the job force providing an occasional diversion or extra spending money. Others may choose a full-time, lifelong career, with a hobby of cooking or needlework as a diversion from the intensity of the marketplace. The important thing to realize is that any given woman may play many roles throughout her lifetime, or she may play only a few roles; but no woman can play all the roles at the same time, and no woman should be placed into an arbitrary role of someone else's choosing.

For in the area of women's roles there is endless potential for legitimate, God-given possibilities. It is imperative for each of us, male as well as female, to have an attitude of openness in viewing the potential as well as the uniqueness of woman's role in life. For the specific role of any one woman will inevitably affect the roles of the men around her, whether they be in the home or in the marketplace. It is also as important for us to become aware of the broad potential for opportunity available to women in this century as to guard against the tendency to get overenthusiastic and try to do it all.

For a long time, up until the recent past, we thought that to be truly woman a woman must be into a career, pushing the more traditional commitments of home and family to

the side. Before that we women as well as the men with
whom we related felt that woman was meant to exist exclusively for the needs of her husband and domestic tasks,
along with childbearing.

During the past two or even three decades many of us
have painfully endured the excesses of the woman's movement, yet we have also seen the positive side in added
opportunities and greater equality for women. Sometimes
the price tag has been too high, such as when women have
burned out trying to do it all or when women have lost their
sense of God-given femininity in trying to become like
men. We had a hard time with the role of domestic chattel,
but we have had an equally hard time with many aspects of
the role of liberated woman.

Yet with the Bible as a basic guideline, what we can
distill out of the past chaos is that woman can be capable
and productive without losing her God-given uniqueness
as a woman. "Women in their 30's are reverting to old-time
values. It's a new morality of the '80's, or maybe a preview
of the '90's . . . This then is the new story—which is really
a new-old story—of getting back to the basics in a culture
of instant gratification, of groping for traditional patterns,
now blurred beyond distinction and wrapped in different
packages." So says an article in the August 25, 1987 *Los
Angeles Times* magazine.

When General Douglas MacArthur was forced by presi-
dential order to leave the Philippines during World War II,
he did it with great reluctance. Going back to the times of
his father, the general had deep roots in the Philippine
Islands. To leave Corregidor in their time of greatest need
and to leave his troops to the almost inevitable slaughter of
the Japanese was against all General MacArthur's instincts

as a man as well as a commander. Yet to refuse to do so would have accomplished nothing except a court-martial. So he left, with the now famous promise: "I shall return!" The people of the Philippines saw that promise as their only hope of deliverance.

Yet as the train carrying the general, his wife, and small son sped through the night to Melbourne, MacArthur paced back and forth in his special car, wondering what really lay ahead. Says biographer William Manchester:

> He sounded like a broken man, and his wife shared his torment. She walked with him until, exhausted, she collapsed on a seat, and even then she remained alert, listening and sympathizing. It was during that long night, she later told a friend, that she resolved to renounce her own private life and live entirely for her husband and son; the general was "a lonely, angry man" who needed her "as never before." By the next morning the general had recovered himself and "looked like business."[1]

But his wife had deepened her commitment; she had declared to herself what was to become her lifelong role.

Jean Faircloth was a tiny southern woman who had met General MacArthur on board a ship. Later, on a Friday morning in April, 1937, they were married. She had married a man who was already a distinguished four-star general. As Manchester states it, from that time on "it seems never to have occurred to Jean that she might have disagreed with her husband about anything."[2] A child was born to them, and for the rest of her life Jean MacArthur made her son and her husband her focus. Even after his death, she refused to grant interviews or write books. Her policy had held her in good stead for over forty years, she claimed, and she wasn't about to change it now. She had chosen a quite singular role, and for her that role was to be for life.

She became the general's primary human support. In so doing she remained in the background, yet always there. After the war was over and MacArthur became the conquering yet much-loved dictator of postwar Japan, Jean was praised by the Japanese people as " 'a symbol of the wifely devotion' " which the Japanese considered " 'a paramount virtue among women.' "[3] They, too, saw the clarity of her role. As the most outstanding general this country has ever produced and as a pivotal force in the outcome of World War II, General MacArthur needed the kind of support he received from his wife. Her role was unique for her at that time and for that particular relationship. Indeed, the whole outcome of the war and the history of mankind itself might have turned out differently without her.

Each woman's role is unique to her. Any woman in her lifetime may play only one major role, or she may play many roles, or even several at one time. What is correct for one woman may not be suitable for another. In this new-old day in which we live, the possibilities for women are endlessly accelerating. For we have indeed come full circle, from an older and at times repressive view of women, through an attitude of so-called liberation, which at times lost as many rights as it gained, to a new-old position that preserves the best of both. Yet in the middle of all these newly developing role choices, the ideal character of every woman remains uniquely constant and seems to be still timelessly expressed in the words of poet William Wordsworth:

> *A perfect woman, nobly plann'd*
> *To warn, to comfort and command;*
> *And yet a spirit still, and bright,*
> *With something of an angel light.*[4]

This still is the epitome of woman. For while her opportunity has expanded and her value is no less than that of a man, she still is uniquely and timelessly woman.

TWO
Choice in a New-Old World

Nine-year old Sara, whom I saw in counseling sessions for a number of months, happily announced to me that she had finally decided that she was smart and that she wanted to become a doctor. Another little girl about two years younger has become committed to the idea of writing books. They are both bright children and even at these young ages seem suited for these professions. Sara has a love for math and a competitive determination that may well lead her into the medical field. Laura, the second child, is perceptive and sensitive and very verbal when she is comfortable in a situation. It has not entered either of their heads that being a woman could be a drawback or that "it's a man's world out there." Rather, they are growing up in families and in a culture where women are uniquely free to develop their vocational interests. Their world is the new-old world of woman. They have known no other.

True, there is still inequality between men and women—

but not as much as there used to be. Little girls are not as apt to grow up thinking that they have to be nurses because they can't become doctors. If they want to be nurses, it's more often than not because that's what they really want to be. They have a choice. Culturally, we women still have conflicting roles at times, but that is better than having one repressive role into which all women are expected to fit.

When one comes from the viewpoint of biblical Christianity, the role of a woman becomes more focused and less confusing. Biblical women were entrepreneurs, judges, homemakers, and Bible teachers, just to mention a few roles. Thus the Christian woman has the clarity of purpose set forth in the Bible, which allows for great potential in the development of ability and shares in the advantages of a society that daily opens doors for women.

With these advantages, however, comes unique responsibility. Women can no longer hide behind discrimination as a cop-out for not doing anything, because discrimination, while it exists, is not usually strong enough to be prohibitive. Nor can a woman claim that as a Christian she should withdraw from any intellectual challenge, for clearly that is not what the Scriptures teach. Today's woman is thus confronted with the choice of becoming what she wants to be—of being uniquely a woman in the way she wishes to fulfill that role.

Alice is in her late thirties. She is married, has three children, and has never worked in a job outside of her home. If she had never married, she probably would have been a commercial artist, since she went to art school and was developing her artistic talents when she met Ken. She still paints, exhibits, and even sells paintings. But her first love is her home and family.

Her home is warm and artistic, and she is a source of refuge and help to many people who stop by for lunch or afternoon coffee. Every Saturday morning she bakes cookies—from scratch! Her lampshades are products of a class she took at the local high school, as is an occasional hooked rug or upholstered chair.

Her children are always put to bed with a story. On rainy days they know that the evening meal will be special and that there will usually be a fire in the fireplace. They've grown used to home-baked food and handmade doll clothes.

Alice has chosen a life-style that suits her and pleases her family. It's right for *her*.

Nicolle, on the other hand, has chosen a very different way of life. She, too, is married; but she is also the editor of a thriving Christian magazine. She is deeply involved in her work and in issues that arise from it. Her viewpoints are balanced and far from fanatical; and she is, without a doubt, a person committed to writing and editing in a way that will have a spiritual impact on people's lives and change them.

Nicolle and Alice are both dedicated Christians, but their life commitments are different. Nicolle couldn't care less if her house is filled with needlepoint done with her own hands, while Alice is largely indifferent to the idea of making a major impact on the world that exists outside of her own family and friends.

Nicolle loves to cook, and she keeps a house that is attractive and comfortable. But when it's a choice between home-baked bread or a good article for her magazine, the article wins out. Michael, her husband, is different, too, from Ken. Mike likes a wife who is involved outside the home and finds that her activities stimulate interesting conversations. He understands, too, that with her outside work she is unable to consistently cook, so he willingly shares in cooking their meals. Nicolle's mother is of an older school of thought and would like Nicolle to settle down and raise children. But in all honesty to herself, Nicolle can't just walk away from a way of life that is important to her. To add children to her already busy life would be unfair to the children, to herself, and to Mike. Someday, perhaps, they will have a child or adopt one. But right now it is not at the top of their priorities.

Claire, on the other hand, is still different from Alice and Nicolle. Claire is also in her thirties, unmarried, and a research scientist with a doctoral degree in bacteriology. Once a few years back she was deeply in love with a heart surgeon. But maybe because both of them were so absorbed in their work, their romance ended.

While at times Claire wishes she had a husband, she values her freedom, too. Her research often sends her to foreign countries, where she works for several months on a project, or on lecture tours within the United States. Her personal life is far from dull. She dates, and she has a variety of female friends as well, including some who are married. As a Christian woman in the field of science she has made valuable contributions in working with student groups on several university campuses. Claire has desires for a home and children, for a husband, for sex; but she has put such a high priority on her professional life that only a very unique marital arrangement could fit with her life-style. Once again, for her this is the life-style she has chosen. It has not been thrust upon her. For choice becomes the responsibility of the new-old view of woman.

Alice, Nicolle, and Claire fulfill distinct and different roles. Of course there are countless women who fit into variations of these roles. The important point is that they have each chosen to shape their lives uniquely. All are definitely feminine. All wish they had time to fulfill a variety of roles. Claire would like to sew. Alice would like to travel more. Nicolle would like to have more time at home than she has with her present life-style. Both Claire and Nicolle think they may want children someday, and sometimes Alice wishes she didn't have any! But all three have been smart enough to know that they can't do everything, and especially not all at once.

With such opportunity for expansion of roles, however, come some inherent conflicts. The power of choice brings conflict. Also, when any one person's role changes, those closely associated with him or her will find that the change also affects their relationship with each other.

Jean came home later than usual one afternoon. After having lunch with her best friend, Marie, picking up the kids at Little League and Boy Scouts, then doing the last-minute grocery shopping, she barely made it home by the time her husband, Peter, walked in the door.

"Can't I ever have dinner on time these days?" he shouted at her. "Why do you have to waste time gossiping with Marie? If you had come home after work and spent the afternoon doing housework and cooking, I would have my dinner and the evening's relaxation that I deserve."

Six months earlier Peter had literally dragged his twenty-eight-year-old wife to my office. "Make her more independent," he begged. "She calls me six times a day at the office; she has no friends of her own; and, frankly, we could use the money if she'd get a part-time job." I explained to Peter that if Jean's self-esteem rose sufficiently, she might also become independent in ways that he didn't like. I stressed the value of both of them coming for counseling, rather than just Jean. But Peter had just brushed that suggestion off, so I had seen Jean once a week alone.

Now it was all beginning to happen. Peter was delighted with his wife's new job. Because she possessed more confidence, he even enjoyed conversing with her more. She seemed to have opinions now and fresh ideas. Yet she certainly wasn't there whenever he wanted her, the way she used to be. He wasn't sure he liked these long lunches and especially the occasional evening out with the girls. Peter had wanted his wife to change, but he had refused to see that the changes in her would demand changes in him and in their relationship.

While the roles of women have expanded greatly, particularly in the years following World War II, when large numbers of women were catapulted by necessity into the work force, the impact of these new roles on male-female interaction is still an area of great confusion.

Susan wasn't even married. She had well-developed work skills. Yet at work her boss wanted her to bring him coffee immediately upon his demand. He asked her to arrange for personal gifts for his friends and family. She made his dental appointments and telephoned for his theater tickets. In general she was his girl Friday, in spite of the fact that none of her male counterparts were ever asked to do these things. They each had the same training and the same job description—but they were of different sexes.

In her personal life, too, Sue's boyfriend expected her to sew on his buttons and help him with certain domestic tasks around his apartment. Yet when they were in her apartment, he expected her to wait on him and would have been horrified if she had asked him to help her with any domestic task. When Sue grew tired of dating and wanted to think about marriage, he reminded her that they were more liberated than that. Marriage was outdated. While he claimed to still believe in Christianity, he preferred to feel that certain teachings of Christ were not for this generation: like marriage and the protectiveness and care that a man is commanded to have toward his wife. Yet he was careful to remind Sue of what he called the scriptural view of women—that of subservience to men.

As women's roles expand it is easy for women themselves to be so grateful for their newly discovered freedom that they try to do it all rather than altering old responsibilities as they add new ones. They tend to avoid making choices. Thus not only do all the various roles conflict, but the woman is left with the feeling that no matter what she does, it will never be enough.

Interestingly, too, as roles shift and change, men also find themselves unsure of how they fit into the scheme of things from a practical point of view. If a woman works full time, for example, she cannot be expected to do all the domestic tasks that were once hers. You can't bake bread, teach the children to swim, have gourmet meals on the table every night at six and still take on the responsibilities of a full-time job.

There is no doubt in my mind that if a man and wife work equally outside the home, they must equally share the tasks within the home. Each will gain and each will lose in this arrangement. There will be more money for both, greater freedom for the wife, and ideally, a more stimulating companion for the husband. But there are negatives. Children will sometimes suffer from the lack of parental nurturing. The husband will often find himself with his hands immersed in soap suds and his evenings filled with changing diapers and taking phone messages for his wife, who may be late, now and then, at the office.

As the man takes over some of the responsibilities of the home, the woman will find that she no longer "calls all the shots" on how the tasks are done. Men have a point when they claim that they avoid picking up their end of the housework because when they do so their wives only criticize them for doing it wrong. Insisting that someone do a task your way is claiming that it is still primarily your task. To relinquish that right is a difficult but necessary step for a woman to take if she wants to alter her role in life and at the same time maintain a positive marital relationship.

Women have had difficulty realizing that with the influx of a large number of new opportunities comes the obligation to make choices rather than to add on an endless list of roles that no one woman can fulfill. With opportunity comes choice, and in the area of choosing roles, choice can at times be painful, for it often means eliminating some roles which are good and attractive in themselves.

Choice means that what may be an appropriate role for one woman may not be satisfactory for another. Choice demands tolerance. It demands a belief that women may perform many good, God-given roles and that no one has the right to think her role is the only legitimate one for a woman. Choice demands acceptance of our roles as God gives us the grace to see them. But that same gift of choice requires a constant evaluation of a role, deciding when it must have alterations in its scope or even when it must change. Above all, choice means that we women must learn to give up certain things in order to have others, for that is the essence of choice.

America's women, married or single, are still in that period of transition in which we have the potential for a variety of roles that are not always clearly defined and that tend to pile on top of each other and end up in conflict because of the lack of a clear-cut choice. We still feel we ought to be able to do it all—and at times we deeply want to do it all. As a result many married women who do not work outside the home feel put down because all they do is cook, clean house, and fulfill their roles as wives and mothers. Single women, too, frequently feel inadequate because, while they may be productive in careers, they are not wives or mothers. Often the single or the married woman will say to the other, "You don't know how lucky you are," because each feels that she has not risen to the expectation of what a woman ought to be. Each feels she ought to be doing it all.

Sometimes the conflicting demands force women into an unreal schedule of pressure and work. A housewife will try to be the perfect wife and mother and excel in a career as well. A woman who is spending a large amount of her time in her career will develop skills in cooking or sewing, even if she dislikes them, because they make her "feel feminine."

One woman I know works full-time, raises four children, bakes her own bread, plays baseball with her son, sews for her three daughters, and literally runs the home, but goes to great pains to make it look to the outside world as though her husband really were the head of the home. She fulfills all her womanly obligations as a wife and mother, and goes on to fulfill much of her husband's role. Then she has to manipulate events so that it looks as if she's just a wife and mother. She's so successful at this game playing that she even fools her own family, and for a while she fooled herself. But until she saw what she was doing and worked on changing it, she was an exhausted, frustrated wreck. Trying to do it all relegates any person to exhaustion and failure. Newfound potential turns into failure and so-called liberty becomes bondage. Freedom to choose one's own way requires the courage to say no to unreasonable demands and the wisdom to know that, even when the choices appeal to us, we can't say yes to all of them.

When I was a single person in my early twenties, I remember walking into the elegantly furnished home of a good friend. Her new baby was adorable, and her husband was attentive. She had all day at home, and she was free to go out to shop and spend her husband's money. *How ideal,* I thought; for at that time I was a young teacher who had to get up early in the morning to go to work and then usually had papers to grade after school. Just as I was about to make a joking remark to that effect, Joy looked at me and said: "You're so lucky; you're free and can do something with your life." Looking at her baby with some rather deep longings of my own, I kept silent. Each of us at that time felt a sense of inadequacy and unfulfillment. Each of us had made a choice, a seemingly good choice for us. But we were failing to enjoy the benefits of that choice, because we were so preoccupied with what we were missing.

Whether a woman is single or married, defining her role can be confusing. Women feel the need to excel, as do men. They study as hard in school, engage in intellectual discussions regarding issues of pertinence to our times, and are in fact thinking, productive human beings. Yet how often on a date or in a marriage do some women still feel obligated to "act dumb," lest they threaten the male ego. Thus the same woman who effectively functions as an intelligent human being at work may pretend to be less intelligent as a wife or a date in order to not appear threatening in a more personal male-female relationship.

Indeed one of the greatest problems arising from the fact that women in our society have been given greater choices and opportunities is that society has still tended to dictate a certain rigid ideal of femininity. In many instances a woman is made to feel that she must marry, raise children, make homemade Christmas gifts, cook gourmet dinners—and then she can be an editor, writer, scientist, social reformer, or anything else she feels inclined toward. No woman can do that. A few may look as if they can. But look deeply into their lives, and you'll find out that it doesn't happen that way.

Femininity is a much deeper issue than baking a cake or dusting a chair. It's an aura that one has. It shows in the way one speaks and looks and responds to people. It's you, as a person. It's not something a woman has to prove by spending so many hours a day doing housework. If a woman chooses to center her life around her home, that's great—for her! It's good because that's what she has chosen to do, not because some artificial cultural standard says she must. For if she is forced by her society to play that role, she will resent it and may largely fail at it.

Part of the reason for the great confusion over the role of a woman in our society is the fast social change that Americans have been undergoing. A century ago the roles were clear. Women were expected to marry, bear children, please their husbands, and keep house. Men were to work all day and provide food, shelter, and protection for their families. Women in general were considered to be inferior in intelligence to men and certainly not as strong.

Yet throughout the history of mankind there have been women who rebelled at their limited position in life. A few real rebels have become famous for their pre–women's-lib activities. Yet there were probably thousands of intelligent women who more quietly endured the injustice afforded

them or fought against it by simply showing their potential
by the quality of the life they lived.

In the mid seventeenth century a remarkable woman
named Anne Bradstreet lived in the Massachusetts Bay
Colony. It has been said that she was a very fine wife and
mother, and she indicated the depth of her spiritual beliefs
when she wrote:

> *The world no longer let me love*
> *My hope and treasure lie above. . . .*[1]

Yet because she showed signs of intelligence and wrote
poetry, she was scorned. In seventeenth-century Massachusetts, women were not supposed to have brains. That
was not part of their role. So she wrote:

> *I am obnoxious to each carping tongue*
> *Who says my hand a needle better fits;*
> *A poet's pen all scorn I should thus wrong,*
> *For such despite they cast on female wits.*[2]

Then as a sort of compromise between her own talent
and potential and her role as a woman at that time, she
continued:

> *Men can do best, and women know it well.*
> *Pre-eminence in each and all is yours;*
> *Yet grant some small acknowledgement of ours.*[3]

In this century woman's roles are broader, if not so clearly
stated as in the time of Anne Bradstreet. In her book
Woman to Woman, Eugenia Price says: "Men have always
been permitted to be people. We have just recently made

it." Singleness, for example, as a choice, not by default, has become acceptable to a degree; yet for both men and women there is still the nagging notion that neither is completely where he or she should be in life, if that person is not married. The same principle holds for pregnancy: No couple is required to have children, but many women feel they have somehow failed at being a woman if they do not bear children.

Thus, although a woman in our society does not have to be married to be accepted, she may frequently feel defensive about her position if she is single. The continued emphasis in most churches on married groups as the norm and singles' groups as marriage mills reinforces the feeling in many single people that for them, as singles, there is no place to fit in with the mainstream of the local church. For some odd reason, too, it seems that a woman who does not marry is believed to have been rejected, an "unplucked flower," or so the saying used to go. Yet men who are single are often viewed as simply not having found anyone yet or as choosing singleness for a career or as possessing some interesting but acceptable streak of eccentricity in their personalities. Thus I have had women tell me that the main reason for their marriage is the social acceptance it brings. Yet such a basis for marriage is far from a scriptural one, when you remember that in the Bible the marriage union is compared to the love relationship that exists between Christ and His church.

Thus the rapid change in women's roles that has occurred in recent years is a major factor in the present conflict concerning these roles. Change has occurred, but we have not assimilated it. Unconscious attitudes and societal ideals conflict. It's all right to be single, but it's not all right. You should be a gourmet cook, but if you're "liberated," you'll use TV dinners. Women can now be the aggressor sexually—but only guardedly. Be independent in the marketplace, but not at home. On and on—we could develop an endless list of paradoxical expectations into which some women still attempt to fit.

At either extreme of the spectrum are the women who avoid the conflict by choosing one radical role and forgetting the rest. But one senses that they, above all, feel frustrated. One completely "liberated" patient of mine and her husband engaged in mate swapping, according to their own individual desires, and in most other areas of their lives they were "equal." They were both totally without obligation to each other. They had their own jobs, cooked their own meals, much like roommates, and had their own friends. Yet the wife sought my professional help because she was a scared, disillusioned woman who was tired of a relationship that cast her into the role of being like a man in every way except sexually. Even sexually she felt dissatisfied, because underneath she really wanted her husband for herself. Her so-called freedom had carried too great a price tag.

At the other extreme, a woman in her late forties was very disturbed because she was nothing but a cook, maid, and sex partner with a man who demanded that she be available every minute of the day.

Both women fulfilled extreme roles. Neither tried to fit in to any of the variety of positive roles that are open to women in this society. Neither decisively chose the role or roles they really wanted. They sort of fell into their life-styles by default or impulse, and neither was happy.

The problem of female roles is a very complicated and confusing one. Even in evangelical Christian circles the role of a woman is not clearly defined with any degree of consistency and is, indeed, often contradictory. I shall never forget a woman missionary, who achieved great acclaim in this country a few years ago, shouting out the words, "Where are the men?" She was specifically referring to a small missionary station in the interior of China, where she had worked for years without seeing a single male missionary. Why was it, she asked, that in America the evangelical male churchgoer usually takes positions of authority in the church. Women have other functions, like cooking, Sunday-school teaching, and child care. Yet no one in the mission home office objected to her being pastor, deacon, or elder as long as she was in the hills of north China!

Within the organized Christian church there is great variety in the viewpoint regarding women's roles. Certain denominations now ordain women as ministers, while others still do not even allow women to speak or pray in a church meeting (although I have never been able to figure out why these same churches allow women to sing solos or why missionary tapes from female missionaries are played in the main church service without compunction). In between these two extremes exists every variation imaginable: A woman can teach, but not be a pastor; she can pray, but not teach; she can pray if she has a head covering.

In contrast to what is true in practice, the organized church, rather than needing to add to the existing confusion over women's roles, has the ability by the use of biblical principles to cut through the confusion and offer a sense of godly balance to the issues. It is my belief that the scriptural view of women's roles is clear and is in no way degrading. Contrary to the view that a woman is some kind of second-rate man, the Bible presents a very high view of women. Building upon this viewpoint, it is possible for the

Christian woman, even in twentieth-century America, to find roles in which she is equal in worth to man yet very different from him in kind. For God's ideal of womanhood is not degrading, neither denigrating her worth nor falsely making her into some cheap imitation of a man. To God, she is a unique individual with capacities that have too long been denied or made light of. In a sense, this new-old view of woman is not new at all. It is just new to our age. For it is actually the way God has always viewed woman.

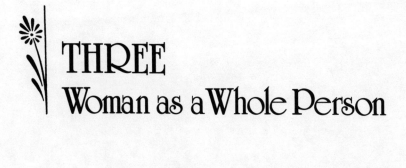

THREE
Woman as a Whole Person

Kathleen was a mother in her middle twenties. Her twin daughters were the delight of her life. When her next child was a boy, it was as though the family was a complete unit. Other children might enhance that unit, but essentially both parents were content.

The only real problem existed within Kathleen herself. Instead of feeling the joy she had experienced after the birth of the twins, she felt increasingly depressed. After fervent prayers for the baby to be a boy, now she felt only a profound sadness, a feeling that at times plummeted to the depths of suicidal despair. Her family and friends were confused and even a little annoyed at her reaction to the birth of this beautiful baby; her doctor claimed she would get over it. No one took her feelings seriously.

Then one bright, spring morning Kathleen brought her twins to her mother-in-law's house, went home with her newborn baby, shut up the house, and turned on the gas. Her mother-in-law was perceptive enough to sense that something was wrong, so help came in time to save both the baby and the mother. However, much pain on the part of all could have been avoided if the family as well as the professional involved had been better equipped in understanding woman as a whole person.

It is important to realize that few of our problems are all physical or all emotional or all spiritual. Some are more physically based than others or more psychologically or spiritually oriented; but more often than not, all three areas merge, and to get help aimed at the whole person is the most effective approach. A duodenal ulcer may be psychogenic, yet it is a real enough physical symptom to cause death. Some cases of diabetes are based on an inherited predisposition to the disease, yet the disorder itself may not manifest itself until the person is exposed to major stress. Many psychiatrists now feel that a person diagnosed as manic-depressive actually suffers from a biochemical disorder. And the great preacher Charles Haddon Spurgeon often referred in his writings to that depression that is part of spiritual warfare and so often accompanies some great success accomplished for God's work.

In "The American Scholar" Ralph Waldo Emerson discusses the paradox of the whole having several parts and yet being one.

It is one of those fables which out of an unknown antiquity convey an unlooked-for wisdom, that the gods, in the beginning, divided Man into men, that he might be more helpful to himself; just as the hand was divided into fingers, the better to answer its end.

The old fable covers a doctrine ever new and sublime; that there is One Man—present to all particular men only partially, or through one faculty; and that you must take the whole society to find the whole man. Man is not a farmer, or a professor, or an engineer, but he is all. Man is priest, and scholar, and statesman, and producer, and soldier.[1]

"To take Emerson's idea one step further, any individual is not divided neatly into three parts but is a total of all three. A loaf of bread is made up of several ingredients such as flour and eggs and milk. Each is distinct from the others, but once they are combined into a loaf of bread, they cease to be distinct and separate. Instead of being eggs, flour, and milk, they become bread. Likewise a person is not three equal parts—body, mind, and spirit—but a whole made up of all three. Yet, in spite of this interrelationship, at times one part may stand out from the others, and here the loaf of bread analogy stops."[2]

In relating the effect of the body on the mind, Charles Spurgeon says in one of his sermons: "Certain bodily maladies are fruitful fountains of despondency. And let a man strive as he may against their influence, there will be hours and circumstances in which they will overcome him."[3] Given the knowledge we have today about the unique metabolic makeup of a woman, Mr. Spurgeon would have been a strong advocate for seeing woman as a whole person. So, too, would the often misquoted and misunderstood Freud, who at one time said: "I am firmly convinced that one day all these disturbances we are trying to understand will be treated by means of hormones or similar substances."[4]

For while men, like women, suffer in common from certain emotional symptoms that actually arise from the malfunctioning of their physical bodies, such as the tension that can be symptomatic of hyperthyroidism, women have a potential for certain biochemical imbalances that are peculiar to them alone. It is vital for us women to realize this about ourselves if we are to function at our full potential. It is also important for men to have some idea of the biochemical makeup of women, if they are to understand us.

To take the example of childbearing, many women experience a sort of euphoria during pregnancy, which some experts feel is due to the increase in the levels of the hormone progesterone. Women in this category often exclaim that they feel better during their pregnancy than during any other time in their lives. Whether a pregnant woman feels good or not, after her delivery, her level of progesterone drops dramatically and in general tremendous hormonal changes transpire. The result may be felt emotionally as well as physically. The much-prayed-for infant may suddenly be unwanted, or at least he or she may become a source of irritation by his frequent demands. The frustration of too many children too soon or general bad nutrition or a poor marital relationship rather than one that offers support are factors that may, of course, exacerbate the situation. But what has too often been ignored in the past is the hormonal base for what we call postpartum depression.

Postpartum depression and its extreme, postpartum psychosis, where the patient is temporarily out of reality, have a real biochemical base that according to some, may be related to the same hormonal imbalance that affects the now-popular and seemingly newly discovered PMS, or pre-menstrual syndrome. According to one expert:

> Some researchers have suggested that an imbalance between the relative levels of estrogens and progesterone in the period immediately following delivery is the trigger; others say there may be a kind of rebound effect—an over-production of hormones—following the loss of the placenta that the body can't handle. The view espoused by Dr. Dalton (the British pioneer in the field) is based on a feast-and-famine analogy. The hormonal swings of the menstrual cycle are infinitesimal compared with the massive increase in placental steroid hormones, including progesterone, during pregnancy and the abrupt deprivation of these hormones following delivery. . . . This dramatic shift in hormone levels results in many women experiencing what's tantamount to an addict going cold turkey: feeling the euphoric glow in late pregnancy, probably caused by the huge amounts of progesterone in the bloodstream, followed by the progesterone deprivation and depths of depression.[5]

Not all women experience the "baby blues." And very few of those who do feel varying degrees of depression go to the extreme of suicide. But some do. Just as women experience varying degrees of PMS.

Most of us women could have told the medical profession a long time ago that there are times in our lives when we notice a certain tension or even depression right before our periods. In some women, however, the condition is more extreme, and the suffering can be great.

As a disorder, PMS includes a group of symptoms that may include fatigue, bloating, irritability, depression, headache, tension, and a craving for sweets. To be diagnosed as PMS the patient must also have these symptoms

in a consistent premenstrual pattern. Even if a woman
does not fit this pattern consistently, most people would
now agree that a woman's menstrual cycle does tend to
include some premenstrual discomfort from time to time.
Taken as that, the symptoms can then be somewhat dis-
regarded and one can go on with one's task, knowing
that it is just that time of month and the symptoms will
soon disappear. For the woman with more severe PMS,
however, the symptoms can range from moderate discomfort to extreme depression or hopelessness, and as
such they require more treatment than psychological
platitudes. In these cases hormone treatment can be
helpful.

Sometimes the symptoms may not entirely fit the clas-
sical definition of what is currently called PMS. One
woman whom I saw in counseling sessions seemed to go
through several menstrual cycles with relatively normal
symptoms. Then the premenstrual tension would start,
and each month the tension would accelerate. In her,
there seemed to be no other premenstrual symptoms, except for what eventually became extreme tension. A physician who was particularly open to new methods and
very sensitive to the feelings of his patients tested her
hormone levels and discovered, after a period of several
cycles, that her estrogen levels tended to become increasingly elevated each month, and the tension would increase. A mild hormone injection seemed to last for
several months; then the cycle would start all over again.
With this fairly conservative treatment the patient experienced normal periods once again, and eventually the
problem diminished and finally disappeared. Because of
the effective medical treatment, her period of counseling
was effective and relatively short-term. Yet it would have
been so easy for her to have assumed that since the

symptom was psychological, the cause must also be psychological.

As a woman approaches the end of her menstrual cycles she once again may experience a unique set of problems concerning the body-mind relationship. Technically *menopause* means "the cessation of the menstrual cycle." This may occur suddenly, with the monthly periods coming to an abrupt halt. Or the cycle may start and stop, with the monthly periods becoming irregular in their timing and with the person even skipping periods from time to time before the periods actually stop altogether. For some women the periods just seem to wind down, becoming shorter in duration and lighter in actual menstrual flow, until one month the cycle stops completely. Whatever the way menopause occurs, it, too, involves a drastic change in a woman's metabolism and may cause symptoms ranging from hot flashes, with their accompanying sweating and chills, to the more psychological manifestations of depression and irritability.

In our present society, our view of age is a negative one. We try to flee from it by the use of cosmetic surgery or by excessive use of extreme diets and sometimes overrated cosmetic treatments, and ultimately we just end up trying to deny that we are growing old, until the reality becomes too obvious in its manifestations for us to keep up the masquerade any longer. To us women all the connotations of aging are wrapped up in one dismal package called menopause. Writer Anne Sexton calls it the "November of the body."[6] Another writer says: "Reminders of mortality, like dunning notices from creditors, provoke reactions as predictable as the plot of a Gothic romance: dread, fear, avoidance, depression, or reluctant confrontation. For women, the start of menopause signals a harsh reality: fertility is drawing to an end, the autumn of life is at hand."[7] The autumn of life is also at hand for men at this age, but since age can make a man simply look more distinguished as opposed to old, and since men can still continue to sire children well into the outset of senility, we women tend to be more acutely aware of the aging process than our male counterparts. Thus for the woman there are many psychological implications in menopause, and some of the symptoms that accompany it, for even years before it actually occurs, may be partially based in the emotions.

However, it is vital for us to understand that once again the hormone imbalances that may occur should not be ignored. Changes in production of the female hormone estrogen can cause physical changes ranging from vaginal dryness to a greater potential for heart attacks, since estrogen tends to protect women from heart attacks during childbearing years. Osteoporosis, causing a brittleness of the bones and thus increasing a woman's chances for the dreaded hip fractures that so often seem to accompany old age, is another vulnerability that connects with lessened estrogen production.

As the body is deprived of its higher estrogen levels there may also be psychological symptoms of depression, crying spells, irritability, anxiety, and short tempers that result from the estrogen deprivation rather than anything in the psyche. Estrogen therapy may alleviate these, and no women should have to endure symptoms that can be alleviated by relatively simple medical treatment.

It is important to note that estrogen treatment may only exacerbate the symptoms of PMS, for which the hormone progesterone can be an effective treatment. Thus it is vital for a woman to be aware of whether her symptoms are cyclical, which would indicate PMS, or whether they occur at random, in which case, taken together with her age, it may be concluded that what looks like PMS may be menopause instead. In those cases where a woman has had untreated PMS and then goes into menopausal symptoms as well, a combination of estrogen and progesterone may alleviate the symptoms. The Bible is not exaggerating when it states that we are fearfully and wonderfully made. Our theology as Christians supports this view, and increasingly medical science backs it up.

To actually tag the condition of premenstrual distress as PMS has meant that professionals now at least have to face it as a verifiable medical problem, and therefore many women can now receive medical treatment. In contrast to such an attitude of openness, I can remember as a junior-high-school student hearing people who ought to have known better, like teachers and school nurses and even some doctors, telling us girls that if we even had such a clear-cut physical symptom as menstrual cramps, it was just because we "resented our periods"! You can imagine what they would have said about PMS, with all its more psychological symptoms like depression and anxiety!

Too often the causes of any hormonally based conditions have been relegated to simplistic, denigrating explanations such as, "She resents being tied down to a baby," or, "She resents being a woman." Or in the case of menopausal symptoms, "She is afraid of growing old," or, "She is experiencing the 'empty nest' syndrome." While certainly psychological factors may be involved, it is also important for women to realize their biochemical uniqueness.

By nature we humans are such extremists. We are like the proverbial blind man who perceives the elephant as being a long, spindly tail or a curved trunk or a great body. To the psychologist, the patient is made up of many neuroses, a bundle of pathology from past life experiences. To the endocrinologist, the problem is glands and their secretions. To the priest, the problem is sin. To the sociologist, the answers lie in society itself.

Of course, these generalizations are grossly overexaggerated and oversimplified, but nevertheless they contain truth. Every woman, while respecting the advice of those professionals whom she consults, needs to realize that they, too, come from their own biases, both professional and personal. It is each woman's obligation to take control of her own treatment to the extent that she asks questions, seeks second opinions when it seems appropriate, and ultimately makes her own decisions. Many professional counselors as well as physicians have a cowardly tendency to excuse their own ignorance and lack of perseverance by relegating everything they don't understand in a person to either psychological problems of unknown origin or even to sin itself. In few areas has this tendency been more true than in the problems peculiar to women, because of their unique hormonal makeup.

Even those in the so-called women's groups who resent the abuse that women have undergone through a lack of understanding by professionals have ambivalent feelings. They want women to have proper treatment for uniquely female problems, yet they hesitate to admit to any biochemical vulnerability that could become a weapon for society against women's ability to handle jobs with the same stability as men. In my opinion these more militant advocates of women's rights can't entirely have it both ways. Yes, there are potential biochemical imbalances that are unique to women. Once again, we are indeed different from men. We can be equal in worth but not in kind. However, these imbalances are often very treatable. The main problem has been to get them recognized for what they are. Men have other vulnerabilities, and I think in the long run they even out. Ultimately stability does not depend on whether or not a person is male or female, but on the individual and his or her strengths and weaknesses.

Related to the problems of PMS, menopause, and post-partum depression are issues like too little sleep or poor nutrition, which can relate to or cause psychological symptoms. The late Dr. Granville Knight, who was a prominent allergist, once stated that even in a condition as common as anemia, where the tissues do not get enough oxygen, a patient may become depressed as well as physically weak. Vitamin deficiencies, too, promote bad mental health. Yet according to orthomolecular psychiatrist Dr. Harvey Ross:

> Too many physicians have attempted to use megavitamins by giving inadequate doses of a few vitamins to the wrong people for an insufficient amount of time only to achieve the failure that could have been predicted. Unfortunately, they conclude that megavitamin therapy is a fraud rather than recognizing that they have not really followed the method as practiced by the orthomolecular psychiatrists. When this is done by an individual practitioner, it is sad enough, but when research physicians make the same error, it is inexcusable.[8]

Another physical problem that can cause psychological symptoms is hypoglycemia. In this condition the person's blood sugar levels become excessively low (as opposed to a disease like diabetes, where the blood sugar levels are abnormally high). Possible symptoms like fatigue, frontal headaches, craving for sugar or alcohol are general enough that it is easy to misdiagnose the condition or to relegate it to a psychological diagnosis, such as depression. Since low blood sugar can be symptomatic of PMS in certain women, a chronic problem of low blood sugar all month will tend to get worse as a woman's monthly period approaches. Thus, while hypoglycemia is a problem in both men and women, it is uniquely a problem for women.

For a while low blood sugar, or hypoglycemia, was an overdiagnosed, overtreated condition, thus damaging its credibility as a viable disorder. Also, many physicians are not precisely trained in either administering or reading a blood test such as the glucose tolerance test or in the actual treatment of low blood sugar itself. Either the disorder is not diagnosed at all; or the results of treatment are poor, and the existence of the disorder itself, rather than the knowledge of the physician, is questioned. Yet when the condition exists untreated, it can make life into a torment.

A young woman sat in my office, complaining of depression. She was a licensed clinical psychologist and was quite sure that she needed some immediate and long-range counseling. The more she talked, something about the whiteness of her face and her profound fatigue made me uncertain in starting counseling sessions without a more thorough medical workup than she had undergone. For I have found in the past that where there is a medical problem contributing to or causing an emotional problem, infinite time, money, and discomfort on the part of the patient can be spared if the medical problem is attended to at the outset.

Sara reluctantly went to a physician who was particularly trained in the area of metabolic imbalances and their relationship to the mind. Even on a random test, her blood sugar count was so low it was a miracle that she hadn't passed out. Within a short time her color was back to normal, and her depression was cut in half. Within six months she was a healthy, happy person. Without that medical treatment, counseling would have been only partially effective at best.

Volumes could be written on the effect of the body on the mind. Every woman and those who deal with women will benefit from an acquaintance with these general areas where the body may be contributing to a woman's emotional and spiritual ill health.

Yet as one becomes aware of the effect of the body on the mind it is vital not to lose perspective on the vast influence the mind still has on the body. A few minutes of anxiety can inflict a period of several hours of exhaustion on the body. It is not uncommon to hear of people who develop asthma attacks during a divorce proceeding or rashes on a first day of school.

In a positive way, too, the mind can affect the body. Those who work with severely ill patients in hospitals can vouch for the effectiveness of hope on a person who may feel that he is dying. A woman who sought my professional help because she was afraid that she had a lot of emotional problems paid me one of the best compliments someone in this field can receive and also illustrated to me the rather dramatic effect of the emotions on the body. When she first entered my office, Margaret was white and had a drawn face. For a while she unloaded a lot of fears that had built up inside her for a long time. Most of them could be put into perspective in a few minutes. A few required several more sessions. But essentially she was a normal woman who had slipped into a temporary period of self-doubt. As I reassured her about her normalcy Margaret's hands relaxed in her lap, and her facial muscles smoothed out. Her color returned, and the edge left her voice. Physically she changed in a positive direction, because she had been psychologically encouraged. She actually *looked* visibly reassured. As she left my office she turned to me and said: "You know, I almost feel that I don't even need professional help!"

In commenting about the positive effects of knowing meaning in one's life, Dr. Viktor Frankl gives an example where such positiveness became actually life-saving:

As for myself, when I was taken to the concentration camp of Auschwitz, a manuscript of mine ready for publication was confiscated. Certainly, my deep concern to write this manuscript anew helped me to survive the rigors of the camp. For instance, when I fell ill with typhus fever I jotted down on little scraps of paper many notes intended to enable me to rewrite the manuscript, should I live to the day of liberation. I am sure that this reconstruction of my lost manuscript in the dark barracks of a Bavarian concentration camp assisted me in overcoming the danger of collapse.[9]

If the effect of the body on the mind has been often ignored and the effect of the mind on the body overemphasized at times, it has also been the sad tendency within the organized church to either spiritualize all problems or to go to the other extreme and forget that our focus and our anchor does still lie in God, no matter how sophisticated our psychological and medical knowledge may become. Hence the importance and yet difficulty of maintaining balance.

Years ago, when I was making the transition from teaching to counseling, one of my gravest concerns about going into this field related to this problem of imbalance. I had seen the cruel devastation resulting from those who overspiritualize, making everything into sin and in so doing causing people who truly love God to even doubt their relationship with Him at a time when they most need Him. What frightened me even more were those people who had once walked with God and who had now all but turned on Him in their worship at the feet of psychology, as though it were some kind of sacred cow. I agreed with God to become a psychological counselor if He would keep me from ever putting my psychological knowledge above my knowledge of Him. I asked for balance, not a balance born out of fear or untruth, but a balance between the truth of biblical Christianity and sound psychology. He has not failed me yet in our pact regarding this matter.

For the purposes of this book, it should not be necessary to explain in any detail that I am not in any way minimizing the innate sinfulness of mankind, the destructiveness of that sinfulness on the lives of all of us, men and women alike, and the efficacy of the grace of God. But as the old hymn so aptly states it:

> . . . We make His love too narrow
> By false limits of our own;
> And we magnify its strictness
> With a zeal He will not own.[10]

We see error, and in an effort to correct it we go to another extreme of error. We see psychologists who do not
do their job well in some way, and we promptly condemn
the whole field of psychotherapy. We hear someone going
to extremes on the subject of self-esteem, where a sort of
self-worship exists, and we move to the opposite extreme
of advocating self-hate, as though hating this despicable
creature, *me*, whom God made in His own image for fellowship with Him, could become some kind of distorted
virtue. Actually having a good self-image in no way conflicts with a realistic view of the innate sinfulness of man.
It does not imply worship of the "old nature" of Romans
6. It simply means what is commanded in the book of
Romans (12:3 based on Wuest translation)—to evaluate
oneself honestly before God, neither overdoing one's vir-
tues nor underplaying one's vices. Such an appraisal motivates change of those things that are unlikable and aims
at a comfortableness with oneself that promotes forgetting oneself and getting on with one's life and God's
work. In the long run, perhaps only as we have the best
self-esteem can we truly become self-forgetful or face our
own shortcomings.

Even in the seemingly simple concept that the treatment
of a woman as a whole person is a sound approach, one
encounters imbalance and, at times, actual danger. "Holistic" medicine rightly aims at just what we have been
discussing—treating the whole person, body, mind, and
spirit. But what every Christian ought to know is that there
are some pitfalls inherent in much that goes on under the
name of holism. There are dangers ranging from practices
involving Eastern meditation to actual involvement of the
practices of the occult itself. Spiritual healing done bla-
tantly in the name of demons, not God, is not unheard of.

Because we in the Christian world are not as deeply trained in the Word of God as we should be, far too often Satan himself successfully deceives even Christians by appearing subtly as an "angel of light."

In an age of shallow Bible teaching and an increased dependence on how we feel as a criterion for decision making, we are ripe for the errors that have infiltrated the church through much of what passes for "holistic" medicine. We believe that what feels good is good, and in that attitude we often expose ourselves to great danger.

All this does not mean, however, that there cannot be such a thing as sound *wholistic* (as I prefer to spell it) medicine. Just because there is error does not mean there is not truth. Once again, to live in godly balance means we take out the error and keep that which is right and helpful. In actuality, often it is because something is valuable, such as treating the whole person, that Satan tries harder to distort it with untruth.

The key to combating such error in the local church is most effectively to be found in the positive area of a clergy who spend hours and even days preparing sermons that teach the Word of God. For a spiritually fed church is more likely to perceive error when it encounters it. This deeper kind of preaching from the clergy, however, will only come about if the local church does not try to make their clergy "walk on water" and be all things to all men. One man or woman cannot teach, pastor, organize, and fund raise. That is why we are told that in the Body of Christ there are many members and many gifts.

True psychology does not negate biblical Christianity. Nor does either the Bible or true psychology discount the value of considering the physical being in the healing of persons. For us women, especially, the consideration of physical needs may be the one missing factor that can make a major difference.

Nor should we ever discount the potential for actual divine intervention, at times, in the affairs of mankind. God, by nature of who He is, can do anything, including the healing of the whole person. Why He chooses to do so at times and not at other times is a question only God Himself can answer, and frequently He chooses not to share that answer with us. Both His power to heal and the fact that He does not always choose to do so are, to me, just greater proofs that He is indeed God. For if I entirely understood His ways, I would myself be God, or He would cease to be God. To me one of the greatest proofs of God's existence lies in His unknowableness.

There are, however, those times when, whether the problem is physical, emotional, or spiritual, God just steps in. I experienced this once in a remote part of Mexico, where there was no medical help available, and God simply healed me. The reasons there were more clearly understandable: I was sick; God wanted me to continue to serve Him for yet a while; and there was no available human help. Usually the reasons are not so clear, and I am sure that even in my case there were other considerations that only God knew. In these areas we must simply trust in the old biblical truth that indeed the God of all the earth shall do right.

Years ago a young New York clergyman by the name of Dr. A. B. Simpson developed a debilitating heart condition that threatened not only his ministry but his very life.

Usually it took him until Wednesday to get over the effects of his Sunday sermons. Climbing stairs or even a slight elevation was suffocating agony.

Dr. Simpson was only thirty-seven when he was told by his physician that he might not have long to live. On his doctor's advice, he went for a long rest to the resort town of Old Orchard Beach, Maine. There he happened into an unusual religious meeting conducted by a Boston physician, Dr. Charles Cullis. Dr. Cullis was then having much success with treating tubercular patients through prayer and common sense measures alone.

Several statements made in the meeting about healing through prayer sent Dr. Simpson back to the Bible to find out what Jesus had to say on the subject. He soon became convinced that Jesus had always meant for His gospel to include healing of the body along with the healing of the mind and the spirit.

In the quiet of his room, Dr. Simpson reviewed his life. He was always struggling for even his minimal needs—for enough health to keep going, for enough ideas and intellectual resources to write talks and sermons, for enough caring about other people. It was almost as if his creed was "Of myself I must do everything." But somehow he always fell short of his objectives. Was God now trying to reach him with a new idea? Had he ever really given God a chance to run his life?

One Friday afternoon shortly after that, Dr. Simpson went for a walk. Since he was always out of breath, he was forced to walk slowly. The path led into a pine wood, and he sat down on a fallen log to rest. All around him was that thick carpet of moss so often seen in the Maine woods. Sunlight filtered through the tall pines, laying striped patterns across the emerald green floor. Simpson pulled out his watch and saw that it was three o'clock.

"All things in my life looked dark and withered," Simpson wrote afterward. "The doctors had made it clear that they could do nothing for me. Intellectual life and spiritual life were also at a low ebb. So there in the woods I asked God to become my life for me, including physical life for all the needs of my body until my life work was done. And I solemnly promised to use His spiritual and physical strength in me for the good of others. God was there all right, because every fiber of my body was tingling with His Presence. He had come to meet me at the point of my helplessness."

A few days later, Simpson took a long hike and climbed a mountain three thousand feet high. "When I reached the mountaintop," he related joyously, "the world of weakness and fear was lying at my feet. From that time on I literally had a new heart in my breast."[11]

After this experience, Simpson went on to live a productive life of preaching and writing, until he died at the age of seventy-six.

When I was going through my family's things at the end of several deaths, I found a short column written again by A. B. Simpson, which my mother or aunt had clipped from an old *Alliance Monthly*. It expresses well the integration of body, mind and spirit as they work together in the total health of any individual. In part it reads:

If you want to keep the health of Christ, keep you from all spiritual sores, from all heart wounds and irritations. One hour of fretting will wear out more vitality than a week of work; and one minute of malignity or rankling jealousy or envy will hurt more than a drink of poison. Sweetness of spirit and joyfulness of heart are essential to full health. Quietness of spirit, gentleness, tranquillity, and the peace of God that passes all understanding are worth all the sleeping draughts in the country. We do not wonder that some people have poor health when we hear them talk for half an hour. They have enough dislikes, prejudices, doubts and fears to exhaust the strongest constitution.[12]

Charles Haddon Spurgeon remains my favorite, however, in his summing up of a godly balance in viewing men
and women as whole beings:

Certain bodily maladies are fruitful fountains of despondency. And let a man strive as he may against their influence, there will be hours and circumstances in which they
will overcome him.

As for mental maladies, is any man altogether sane? Are
we not all a little off balance? Some minds appear to have a
gloomy tinge essential to their individuality. . . .

These infirmities may be no detriment to a man's career
of usefulness. They may even have been imposed upon him
by divine wisdom as a necessary qualification for his peculiar course of service.

But where in body and mind there are predisposing
causes to lowness of spirit, it is no marvel if in dark mo-
ments the heart succumbs to them. The wonder in many
cases is—and if inner lives could be written men would see
it so—how some keep at their work at all and still wear a
smile upon their countenance. Grace has its triumphs and
patience its martyrs, martyrs none the less to be honored
because flames kindle about their spirits rather than their
bodies, and their burning is unseen by human eyes. . . .[13]

Viewing woman as a complex being—body, mind, and
spirit, uniquely made in the image of God in order to fellowship with Him and serve Him—lends itself to an attitude of humility and respect for ourselves as women. In our
view of others, to say "Who knows what problem I would
have if I had been this person who is hurting?" is a much
more humble and accurate—to say nothing of godly—attitude than one that tells them to "repent of their depression." How this latter attitude, displayed by those who claim

to serve Him, must grieve the heart of the One who wept over Jerusalem and longed to take them under His wings and comfort them.

One of the deepest regrets of my life relates to my aunt Ruth. When China closed its doors to foreign missions, my aunt came home, broken in body, menopausal, displaced, suffering from cultural shock and deeply concerned over the fate of those Chinese Christians whom she had deeply loved. She never totally seemed to recover. She became well enough to spend some years in Formosa and to start a Chinese mission in the slums of Los Angeles, but she always missed China.

During a particularly down period for her, I was in college and had not yet learned the balance I have spoken of in this chapter. In those days, I tended to overspiritualize situations; and while I was always a very compassionate person, my solutions for people's problems did not always turn out sounding very compassionate. In essence, my advice to my aunt was for her to "confess her depression." Oh, I said it differently, more nicely than I hear some say it today. I couched it in the theology of Romans 6, not realizing that for all my teaching on that chapter I was distorting its real meaning. But the message was there: Her depression was sin. Needless to say, my advice was not very productive.

I have learned from such an experience something of the need for balance in dealing with people's lives. As I sit here at my desk, staring at the screen of my word processor, I can glance up at a picture of my aunt, sitting on a log in the hills of north China, holding a Chinese baby and a little white lamb. I wonder where that baby is today. She would be about my age. I wonder about all those people my aunt led to God in those remote regions.

I wonder about their children. And I know that my aunt did an eternal work for God. Somewhere in the middle of that great cloud of witnesses of Hebrews 12, I believe she knows that I grew from knowing her and watching her pain and that I now help people who suffer as she did. Just as important, she helped me to understand myself as a woman, as a whole person.

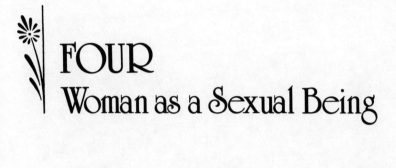

FOUR
Woman as a Sexual Being

"My husband always wants to try different things in our sex life. We very seldom use words to express our love. All tenderness seems gone, and in its place has come an increase of what I call 'kinky sex.' Then last night, when Mark wanted to rent a video film to stimulate us while we made love, I just went hysterical and said that if he couldn't be turned on by me without some pornographic film, he could forget having sex with me at all."

With these words an attractive woman in her early thirties opened up her first counseling session with me. For Jill and her husband, Mark, sex had ceased to be an expression of love and indeed had begun to resemble something closer to a competitive sport. Mark and his jogging buddies had begun to compare the "new" sexual experiences they had just had with their wives; and once someone else had come up with something new or a little out of the average, all the others felt compelled to compete and outdo him. To them sex had become a game more than an expression of love, and certainly it had long left the arena of godliness.

A little girl, five years old, sat on the floor in my office, playing with some small wooden dolls and a toy dollhouse-type village. Suddenly she looked up at me and said with the understanding of a much older person: "Sex is a terrible thing, isn't it?" Carrie had been brutally molested for at least a year of her life; and for her, sexual behavior that she did not even yet understand had been thrust upon her with an ugliness and brutality that had precipitated the question, which she now asked for the first time in my office. She was only five, but I gave her an adult answer: "Sex is a wonderful gift from God, but only if it is between two adults whom God has brought together in marriage. For you, Carrie, it was different," and I went on to explain that difference.

I could not help but think, as I talked to this little girl and later as I have talked to married adults with a mechanistic sex life, of the magnificent portrayal of the marriage union that we are given in that ancient Old Testament book the Song of Solomon. According to the well-founded fantasy of Dr. Harry Ironside, former pastor of the Moody Church in Chicago, a wonderful love story is the underlying thread running through this small Old Testament book, and I feel his fantasy is worth quoting here at some length in order for the reader to get the feel for this remarkable little book on conjugal love. Says Dr. Ironside:

> Up there in the north country, in the mountain district of Ephraim, King Solomon had a vineyard (we are told that in the 11th verse of the last chapter), and he let it out to keepers, to an Ephraimite family. Apparently the husband

and father was dead, but there was a mother and at least
two brothers, two sons. We read, "My mother's children
were angry with me." In Hebrew it is, "My mother's sons."
There may have been more sons, but there were at least
two. And then there were two daughters, two sisters, a little
one spoken of in the 8th chapter—"We have a little sister."
She was a little undeveloped one. And then there was the
older daughter, the Shulamite. It would seem as though
this one was the "ugly duckling," or the "Cinderella" of the
family. Her brothers did not appreciate her and foisted hard
tasks upon her, denying her the privileges that a growing
girl might have expected in a Hebrew home. "My mother's
sons were angry with me." That makes me wonder whether
they were not her half-brothers, if this were not a divided
family.

"My mother's sons were angry with me; they made me
the keeper of the vineyards; but mine own vineyard have I
not kept." They said to her, "No; you can't loll around the
house; you get out and get to work. Look after the vineyard." She was responsible to prune the vines and to set the
traps for the little foxes that spoiled the vines. They also
committed to her care the lambs and the kids of the flock.
It was her responsibility to protect and find suitable pasture
for them. She worked hard, and was in the sun from early
till late. "Mine own vineyard have I not kept." She meant,
"While working so hard in the field, I have no opportunity
to look after myself." What girl is there that does not value
a few hours in front of the looking-glass, the opportunity to
fix her hair and to beautify herself in any lawful way? She
has no opportunity to care for her own person, and so she
says, "My own vineyard have I not kept." I do not suppose
she ever knew the use of cosmetics of any kind; and yet as
she looked out on the road she would see the beautiful
ladies of the court riding on their palfreys and in their
palaquins, and as she got a glimpse of them, or as she bent

over a woodland spring and saw her own reflection, she
would say, "I am sunburned but comely, and if I only had
the opportunity, I could be as beautiful as the rest of them."
That is all involved in that expression, "Mine own vineyard
have I not kept."

One day as she was caring for her flock she looked up,
and to her embarrassment there stood a tall and handsome
stranger-shepherd, one she had never seen before, gazing
intently upon her, and she exclaimed, "Look not upon me,
because I am black, because the sun hath looked upon me."
And then she gives the explanation, "My mother's children
were angry with me; they made me the keeper of the vineyards; but mine own vineyard have I not kept." But he
answers quietly without any offensive forwardness, "I was
not thinking of you as swarthy and sunburnt and unpleas-
ant to look upon. To my mind you are altogether lovely;
behold, thou art fair, my love; there is no spot in thee." Of
course that went a long way toward a friendship, and so
little by little that friendship ripened into affection, and
affection into love, and finally this shepherd had won the
heart of the shepherdess. Then he went away, but before he
went, he said, "Some day I am coming for you, and I am
going to make you my bride." And she believed him. Probably no one else did. Her brothers did not believe him; the
people in the mountain country felt she was a poor simple
country maiden who had been deceived by this strange
man. She had inquired of him where he fed his flock, but he
put her off with an evasive answer, and yet she trusted him.
He was gone a long time. Sometimes she dreamed of him
and would exclaim, "The voice of my beloved," only to find
that all was quiet and dark about her. But still she trusted
him.

One day there was a great cloud of dust on the horizon
and the country people ran to see what it meant. Here came
a glorious cavalcade. There was the king's bodyguard and

the king himself, and they stopped just opposite the vineyard. To the amazement of the shepherdess, the royal out-
riders came to her with the announcement, "The king has
sent us for you." "For me?" she asked. "Yes, come." And in
obedience she went, and when she looked into the face of
the king, behold, the king was the shepherd who had won
her heart, and she said, "I am my beloved's and his desire is
toward me."[1]

The portrayal of love in the Song of Solomon is certainly
neither intellectualized onto some lofty plain that ignores
physical pleasure, nor is it overspiritualized. Indeed, because of its bluntness regarding the physical body, Jewish youths were not allowed to read this book until they
were thirty years old. Its references to the human body
are explicit. There is every indication that sexual union
is considered pleasurable rather than "something a
woman must endure" (an older viewpoint still held by
some) and that it transcends the purpose of mere procre-
ation. While there are various other levels of interpretation to be found in this book, such as the portrayal of
Christ's relationship to the church, certainly at a basic
level sexual activity is presented in its purest sense: pleasurable expression of love toward a person in a relationship legitimatized by the bonds of marriage. Says Hudson
Taylor in his excellent book on the Song of Solomon,
Union and Communion: "He takes delight in her beauty,
but that is not so much the cause as the effect of His
love, for He took her up when she had no comeliness.
The love that has made her what she is, and now takes
delight in her, is not a fickle love, nor need she fear its
change."[2] How many women, and even men, today
would like to be able to have that kind of confidence in
the love of their spouse!

Having established, however, biblical approval for the physical enjoyment of sexual activity, it is important to put that truth into perspective. Women are as much sexual beings as are men, and it is far too easy for women to underplay their own needs and for men to be seemingly unaware of those needs. Such an attitude is shown in statements like: "You must just give him what he wants and not worry about whether or not your needs are met," or, "Women are meant, above all, to meet a man's needs physically." Advice such as this is frequently offered in the guise of being biblical, as portraying a godly view of the submission of a married woman. Actually this viewpoint is far from the truth. Not only does such an attitude ignore the needs of a woman, but because the sex act is then relegated to the meeting of *only* physical needs, it becomes mechanical and meaningless to both parties. Relationships such as these deteriorate into emptiness, glued together by duty and crude, mechanistic sex—no love, no tenderness, with the female body as a sort of machine with which to satisfy male needs.

Actually the portrayal of woman as a chattel who exists for her husband's pleasure feeds very well into a totally worldly viewpoint, where either the woman exists only to meet her husband's needs or where both men and women exist solely for each other's sexual delight. At that point it is a short step to a position where commitment and marriage are considered inconvenient and unimportant. For once a man ceases to love his wife as Christ loves the church, and once a woman ceases to delight in her husband, whether or not he can get an erection at any given moment, the fabric of the marriage is gone and sex, which is supposed to be the expression of love, not merely an orgy of feeling, has no meaning.

Fundamental to such a distorted view of sexuality is a distorted view of marriage itself. A woman is not a bond-slave to her husband. She is in every way equal to him in worth, but very different in kind. She is not "like a man." She is a woman and as such is entirely different from a man. Thus the marital relationship is one of equality of worth, yet it involves the blending of two people with distinct differences within their personalities and roles.

Great confusion exists within the church over the issue of submission within a marriage, and out of a misunderstanding of the meaning of this term a great deal of bondage has existed for Christian women who are married.

According to Dr. Ironside, the words "submit yourselves" in Ephesians 5:22 are not in the best manuscripts. Rather the Greek states it as: "Submitting yourselves one to another in the fear of God, wives unto your own husbands, husbands loving your wives." Continues Dr. Ironside:

> He is not calling upon the wife to take the place of a slave—she often takes that place in pagan lands—but he is calling for mutual loyalty, mutual respect, mutual submission. Pass over the intervening words to verse 25, "Husbands love your wives, even as Christ also loved the Church, and gave Himself for it." That is how the husbands submit themselves unto the wives, so it is a mutual thing. That which makes the Christian home what it ought to be is this mutual loyalty, the one to the other, the wife to the husband, the husband to the wife. This is a marvellous thing when you think about it.[3]

The Expositor's Bible continues with the same emphasis. Again, in reference to Ephesians there is the idea of mutual submission rather than the submission of the wife to the husband only: "Being in subjection to one another in fear of Christ. . . ."[4] Then the writer goes on to explain the equality inherent in a truly godly marriage: "A free and sympathetic obedience—which is the true submission— can only exist between equals."[5] When a marriage is this soundly established, it would be easy to then conceive of the solidity of that marriage which is portrayed by the biblical scholar Dr. Adam Clarke in his exposition of Matthew 19:5:

> [*For this cause*] Being created for this very purpose, that they might glorify their Maker in a matrimonial connection. *A man shall leave* (. . . *wholly give up*) both *father and mother*—the matrimonial union being more *intimate* and binding than even parental or filial affection;—and shall be *closely united . . . shall be firmly cemented* to his wife. A beautiful metaphor, which most forcibly intimates that nothing but *death* can separate them: as a *well-glued board* will break sooner in the *whole* wood, than in the *glued* joint.[6]

In my opinion, most people who seek help with the sexual problems in their marriage need help in areas like self-esteem and communication rather than actual sexual counseling. There are clear-cut exceptions to this statement, of course. But how often I have seen people sort of fall into a better sex life after they have begun to learn mutual respect or begun to talk to their spouses or after they have developed a respect for themselves that flows over into a fuller acceptance of their physical bodies. Their problems were not sexual. An unsatisfactory sex life was just one of the symptoms of other, more pervasive, problems.

Fundamental to a good sex life is an attitude of consideration and mutual respect. "Being in subjection to one another in the fear of Christ" is a good start. I have often thought that if two human beings focused on giving love rather than receiving it, most couples' sex lives would be serene, and the world would certainly be a happier place in which to live. From a human point of view this is an impossible, idealistic goal. But we Christians are different, at least in our potential: We have the love of God resident in us, in that Christ Himself lives in us. Therefore, we have the resources to experience such love.

To borrow Dr. Vernon McGee's term and put this into *shoeleather,* such love would cause both mates to discuss their sexual needs with each other and then to put aside what was offensive to either party. It would also motivate each person to at least try to meet the other's needs in the way he or she likes. From a woman's point of view, love means I try to give my husband what he desires. Love means I accept his dislike regarding certain sexual behavior and therefore do not demand it from him. Love means I respect this person whom I love enough to not insist upon sex when the timing is bad for him. Love means that I do not avoid sex with fake excuses. Love means that I use my sexual behavior to the glory of God and to the uplifting of my spouse, not just for my own self-indulgence. Above all, love does not cease to exist if sexual activity is suddenly rendered impossible. Obviously, in a true love relationship the standard for man would be equally high. Nor is such a standard exclusively Christian. To a large degree it is also just good psychology. For truth is truth, whether it is psychological or spiritual, and it does not conflict with itself.

Dr. Viktor Frankl confirms these concepts of love from a psychiatric point of view:

> True love in and for itself needs the body neither for arousal nor for fulfillment, though it makes use of the body for both. Arousal in a man of healthy instincts is stimulated by the partner's body—although his love is not directed toward the partner's body . . . for the real lover the physical, sexual relationship remains a mode of expression for the spiritual relationship which his love really is, and as a mode of expression it is love, the spiritual act, which gives it human dignity. We can therefore say: as the body is for the love the expression of the partner's spiritual being, the sexual act is for the love the expression of a spiritual intention.[7]

Another noted psychotherapist, Dr. Rollo May, aptly states what will happen if love does not accompany sexual activity. Explains Dr. May:

> If we can have sex without love, we assume that we escape the daimonic anxiety known throughout the ages as an inseparable part of human love. And if, further, we even use sexual activity itself as an escape from the commitments eros demands of us, we may hope to have thus gained an airtight defense against anxiety. And the motive for sex, no longer being sensual pleasure or passion, becomes displaced by the artificial one of providing identity and gaining security; and sex has been reduced to an anxiety-allaying strategy. Thus we set the stage for the development of impotence and affectlessness later on.[8]

Many people who experience sexual dissatisfaction are trying to find an escape in sex, a thrill, a sense of being, and even a place to hide. All these are sometimes a fringe benefit of a good sex life. But still the primary focus of sex is the expression of love. Not cheap, demanding love. But real love that gives. I have seen people who keep charts on the sexual progress of their mates. I have seen sex distorted into a consuming orgy that becomes the focus of the entire life. I have seen potentially good marriages destroyed because one mate was overly self-indulgent in his or her demands or because another mate was too introspective and selfish to give to the other. For the selfishness can go in either direction: demanding too much or giving too little. When sex is based on something other than love, pornographic reading, videotapes, and endless experimentation begin to enter the picture. Sex becomes meaningless and focused on physical sensations alone; and often any mate will do, as long as he or she is innovative and available.

At this point of mechanistic sex many people develop problems. In essence they are so afraid of not performing well that they can actually become unable to perform. And if such a person's mate is as mechanistic in his or her sex life as the one who has this trouble, the lack of performance will be met with disapproval and rejection, which will only increase the problem. For fear of not performing is one of the most common causes of such sexual problems as impotence.

A middle-aged woman once came to me for counseling and complained about her husband's impotence. "He makes me so mad," she exclaimed. "He wants sex, and then he can't even get an erection!" When I questioned her further about how she handled the situation, the solution to the problem became more apparent. Keeping in mind that the man was into middle age and could be suffering from a hormonal imbalance, it seemed obvious that his main problem might be a wife who had always wanted more sex than her husband. She would phrase her demands with threatening statements like: "Well, of course, if it's too much for you. . . ." Or she would taunt, "You know I could get this somewhere else, if you can't do it." Increasingly her demands and threats set up an atmosphere of fear of not being able to perform. Finally he couldn't perform, and then her threats, which increased even more, made him unable to recover. Yet if fear can turn off a sexual relationship, reassurance and real love can often be the best antidotes. For very often a loving mate is the most effective therapy for short-term sexual dysfunction.

Female sexuality, however, is more than sexual activity. It is a feeling, an attitude, a way of moving about and being. Very early in life children develop a sexual identity. For that reason I'm not too keen on the recent phase of trying to force little boys to play with dolls and girls to prefer trucks. While there is nothing wrong with a boy having a doll or a girl a truck, both do better with a majority of toys that basically relate to their own sex. Somehow we women have been brainwashed into equating equality with sameness. I don't have to dress like a man or walk like a man to be equal with him. Nor do little children who are in those important formative years where they are actually developing whom they will be for the rest of their lives need to be confused with unisex toys and clothing.

For a woman, part of being a sexual being is to feel comfortable with her femaleness, to embrace it, so to speak. Bubble baths, my favorite cologne, new purses with a soft leather smell, ruffled sheets, candlelight suppers, holding a tiny baby and watching its fingers curl around my thumb, baking bread or making soup from scratch on a rainy day, dressing in a soft, lacy nightgown and crawling into a bed with fresh, flowered sheets, serving a gourmet dinner with my best china and silver and my mother's lace cloth from China: All these are just the tip of the iceberg of my own personal sense of femininity.

None of this is to be interpreted to mean that men cannot enjoy fine china or that women must like ruffled sheets. Let us not forget that most of the world's greatest chefs are men, not women. To the contrary, this is just a small cross section or sample of my own femininity. For each woman's sexual identity goes much deeper than these superficial things. Because of my own choices in life, choices that have been right for me and that I do not regret, I have never conceived, carried, given birth to, and raised a baby. Somewhere deep inside me there is a deep ache that I rarely talk about when I see babies or baby clothes or maternity clothes or pregnant women. Those feelings are a deeper part of that sexual part that is *me*. The composite of characteristics, longings, and feelings that make up *me,* a woman with female sexuality, will differ from the composite of any other one woman. But women taken as a group will more greatly resemble each other than they will men taken as a group. The differences will tend to be superficial, like a desire to be an auto mechanic or an apathy regarding dolls as a child, and the similarities will be of a deeper sort.

It is important for a woman to see herself as a whole person in this area and not to form fast, superficial judgments based on one or two characteristics that do not fit the norm. For within the broad spectrum of defining what is female and what is male, there is a broad scale of possibilities and exceptions.

Singleness, too, does not make a woman less of a sexual human being, for that composite of characteristics that make her female will still be there. For the single Christian woman, however, there will be a problem with the physical outlet for that sexuality. It is imperative to remember, too, that every married woman is single for a part of her life. She is single before she gets married; she is single if she is divorced or widowed. Therefore, woman as single and yet a sexual being is an issue that must concern all women and should be of great concern to the organized church as it functions in its outreach to women.

Biblically, sex outside the marriage vows is not allowed. For the woman who never marries, this involves the loss of a part of being a woman that is very satisfying. For the woman who does marry, following this injunction will probably be an issue for a part of her life, either before or after her marriage, or at both times.

Contrary to the myth that unmarried women are some kind of "unplucked flowers," somehow never chosen to be anyone's mate, singleness has become increasingly a matter of choice for many women. Currently in this society singleness is a respectable, viable choice. Our economic system makes it very possible for a woman to support herself, so she can afford to choose singleness. As in the case of the Apostle Paul, sometimes a woman may choose singleness in order to do a work, whether it be a consuming task in some secular area, like medical research, or whether it be a God-ordained work that requires a total focus. Sometimes a woman simply does not find the mate with whom she wishes to spend her life, or she finds him but he is not available, for one reason or another.

For the Christian woman or man who chooses single-ness, there is the accompanying biblical command to be celibate. That this is a difficult command goes without saying. Indeed it seems not only difficult to follow, but to do so seems a very large sacrifice of obedience to God.

A while back, when the archbishop of the Catholic Church in Los Angeles retired, he was interviewed briefly on the evening news. He was asked about the sacrifice he had given to God by giving up marriage in order to become a priest in the Catholic Church. I will never forget the essence of his reply and still more the feeling he conveyed with it. His answer was simple: He had been given what he called the "gift of celibacy" in order to serve God; and that lifetime of serving God had been something that had been a privilege, a decision he had never regretted. It had been an honor. The *gift* of celibacy, not the sacrifice! I felt that somehow we Protestants had missed something of the joy of God and serving Him. We view as sacrifice, something even to conceal, as though it were a disgrace, what this archbishop saw as a gift.

Even apart from Christianity, sex outside marriage is not a completely satisfactory answer. Inherently a woman interprets intercourse as an act that means a permanent relationship. When it does not prove to indicate more than a short-range affair, a woman may feel deeply re-jected and unlovable. For the Christian woman there are added problems of guilt and feelings of spiritual alien-ation from both Christian friends and God. One woman I

know who has been sexually involved with a married
man has given up all her Christian friends, because she
can't face them. Another can't feel free in her devotional
life with God, because she is in direct conflict with His
will. Any of the women whom I have talked to who are
having premarital or extramarital affairs and who are
evangelical in their beliefs seem to have lives of carefully
contrived secrecy, which are not conducive to good mental health.

Yet women who have no sexual outlet still have God-
given sexual needs. Constructive busyness, helping others,
creative activities may help, but they are far from complete
answers. Knowing that sexual needs are real and right and
certainly nothing to be ashamed of helps, too. No woman
should feel guilty over having healthy sexual needs. The
married woman who said to me, "Sex is something women
have to endure," was not expressing a healthy viewpoint,
but rather a very repressive attitude. In contrast, a woman
who accepts her femininity and has access to her feelings
will feel sexual needs that will be present even when there
is no desire to conceive a child and no marriage partner
available.

While some Christians are strongly opposed to the idea of
sexual fantasies, others feel that at times they may be a
partial answer for those who have no legitimate sexual
outlet available. The following verse may present a problem
for those who do have fantasies but feel guilt regarding
them. "Anyone who even looks at a woman with lust in his
eye has already committed adultery with her in his heart"
(Matthew 5:28 TLB). But in speaking of this text, Dr. Paul
Tournier says of a single man who felt guilt over his imag-
ination: "I have pointed out to him the obvious fact that this
text did not apply to him, since he was a bachelor, or at

least did not apply to him unless his glance led him to covet a woman he knew to be married."

Furthermore, in considering the text in Matthew, the interpretation of the word *lust* seems pivotal. The same Greek word is translated "desire," "covet," and "lust" throughout the New Testament, and its meaning does not always relate to sex. Rather, according to James Strong's concordance the word means "to set the heart upon, long for." In *A New and Concise Bible Dictionary* it is translated "to desire earnestly."

In Matthew 13:17 (TLB) Christ says: "Many a prophet and godly man has *longed* to see what you have seen. . . ." In 1 Timothy 3:1 Paul says: ". . . If a man desire the office of a bishop, he *desireth* a good work." Galatians 5:17 reads: "For the flesh *lusteth* against the Spirit, and the Spirit against the flesh. . . ." And again in Acts 20:33 Paul says: "I have *coveted* no man's silver, or gold, or apparel." All these verses use the same Greek word (I have italicized their translation) as is used in Matthew 5:28. None of them have sexual references, and all indicate strong desire to the point of action. For example, when Paul speaks in Acts about not coveting their gold, I'm sure he is not saying that he wouldn't like it; he is saying something much stronger, that he doesn't covet it, wish for it to the point of dwelling on it in his thoughts and perhaps stealing it. Thus when Christ speaks of lusting after a woman, the thought is not so much that of a passing sexual fantasy, but something stronger.

The rightness and wrongness of sexual fantasies have been the subject of some controversy, and for each individual woman a decision must ultimately be made between herself and God. In the area of sexual fantasies, the answers are not clear-cut, for the Christian world it-

self has varying opinions, ranging from "Allow your imag-
ination to go in any direction you desire," to "All daydreaming and certainly all sexual thoughts are sinful."
Most of us are somewhere in that broad middle ground
between. From Matthew 5:28 it seems clear that at some
point in their intensity it is wrong for these fantasies to
be directed toward a married person. For the single
woman, however, when the fantasies are directed toward
a single man, they may well provide a partial release of
sexual feeling as well as contribute toward a greater acceptance of personal sexuality in general—something
many Christians have tried to repress in a mistaken attitude that sexuality is somehow sinful. Perhaps for the
single person, too, there will be a point at which the
strength of the fantasy will become too great and an individual may feel wrong in continuing with it. This again
is a matter of degree, and it is up to the individual conscience of the person involved.

As a postscript relating to those who are against all
daydreaming and sexual fantasies, it is interesting to note
that in wholesome secular and even religious literature—
short stories, novels, and movies—the fantasies of other
people are given for our enjoyment, an enjoyment often
based on sexual attraction and readily accepted by most
Christians.

Masturbation is another area of controversy among
Christians, which affects women both single and married,
although once again, as with sexual fantasies, it is probably
of more concern to single women than to those who are
married. In spite of the mythology surrounding the subject,
masturbation is not physically destructive or necessarily
psychologically damaging. Yet it often seems to cause a

tremendous amount of guilt among Christians, and children in particular are often warned severely against it. In one Christian school a teacher told a group of teenagers that they would lose all self-control if they engaged in masturbation. Others have been told they would go insane. I have talked to young people as well as older people who felt that this was the worst sin they had ever committed and that they could have no real relationship with God because of it.

These attitudes, however, are not unique to Christians alone—at least a few generations back! According to an article in *Human Behavior* magazine, "Some procedures that actually were used for masturbators were clitoridectomy (excision of the clitoris) in girls and women and circumcision and deenervation of the nerves leading to the genital area in boys and men." The article goes on to say, "Nowadays, we tend to treat masturbation as normal. . . ."

As is true of most things, masturbation can be used to excess. It can be an excuse for a woman who is avoiding some real problems that exist in her marriage, and as such is psychologically damaging for a woman who has the availability of a legitimate sex partner, yet chooses masturbation instead. For ultimately sex is meant to be an expression of love toward another person. Masturbation can also be used to excess by an adolescent who does not want to get out and deal with social situations in the real world. Thus it seems to me that the morality of masturbation is not so much a matter of black and white, right and wrong, but a matter of degree and timing.

In the day in which we live, human sexuality is of particular concern to women. We worry about our own sexuality as well as that of our spouses and friends. We are obsessed with whether or not we are sexually competent and desirable. We want our independence while we worry about our possible loss of femininity. Role changes for women, role reversals between men and women, where men take on domestic tasks and women become the primary breadwinners, magazine articles that focus on sexual activity as though it were a new national competitive sport, and many other factors have probably made us the most sex conscious and concerned group of people in the history of mankind. We fear sexually transmitted diseases, as well we might, since we as a people participate so actively in sexual relations that frequently are not restricted to just one mate.

Not long ago a woman who has a good marriage but who struggles to keep it that way said to me: "Before we were married, John and I made a vow to each other that each of us would always give one hundred percent to each other when we made love, even if we didn't think that the other person was living up to his or her promise of one hundred percent." She concluded: "Now, every time I get discouraged about our sex life, I just give that hundred percent. I don't keep a tally sheet, but somehow I seem to get back more than I give, at just the times when I'm really not looking for it."

This couple has found a major key to a successful marriage. For this woman it has meant a sex life that depends only on her willingness to give. Psychologists would call it using paradoxical intention to deflect anticipatory anxiety. But you see, with her it's not a technique. It's something as simple as love.

Ideally sex is perfected by just what she is doing: the giving of oneself for one's spouse. It is giving, not taking. In our fight for women's rights and in our understandable desire for equality, we women have sometimes forgotten that we can't negotiate or legislate love and that sexuality transcends the ERA. It goes back to a simple maiden in King Solomon's vineyard, who captured the heart of the king.

FIVE
Woman as Nurturer

"I'm going to have a baby," Susan said with a look of ecstasy. It was not an unusual announcement in itself, nor was it a statement that would normally require more than a few brief words of congratulations on the part of the counselor. This time it was different, however, for both of us.

Ten years previous to this pregnancy Susan and her then three-week-old baby had found themselves virtually alone in this world after the death of Susan's husband in a military plane accident. Jim, her husband, was a test pilot, and even though Susan had always known that Jim lived constantly with the threat of death, when he died, she was unprepared both emotionally and materially.

After a tumultuous two years, Susan remarried. Her new husband, Marc, was a successful physician who deeply loved and admired his new wife. He adopted two-year-old Tricia and loved her as his own.

Deep within both Susan and Marc, however, was the desire to have more children, particularly to have children issuing forth from their own marital union. None came. Friends prayed and advised them to pray harder. "God hasn't answered our prayers" was their conclusion after several years of trying.

A bitterness set in, particularly in Susan. The tapes of "why not" and "what if" began to play. Then, realizing the destructiveness of her attitude, Susan decided to turn away from her focus on babies and do something to help other people's children who were homeless and in need. The bitterness remained and with it a distance from God; but at least the focus changed. Once again Susan's life took on meaning.

During the next eight years many children poured through their home: babies, teenagers, handicapped, healthy. But all had one thing in common: They needed a home and a lot of love and care. Some of the children were brought in to see me for counseling. Some stayed on in the home and were adopted, until it seemed that their family might indeed be a large one after all.

Then one day Susan came in to see me. In an opening remark she said: "You know, maybe I'll never get pregnant, but it's okay now. I need God more than I need a baby. I only want to get pregnant if it's God's will." Six weeks later she was back in my office, telling me about her pregnancy.

To me it seemed that God had rewarded her relinquishment and her faithfulness in working with other people's children. Yet having said that, let us each make sure that we understand that the ways of God are inscrutable. The God of all the earth will indeed do right, and

God is certainly no man's debtor. But that does not mean
that perfectly godly women may not go through life barren; and some pretty unworthy people, at least from our
human point of view, seem to get pregnant with no effort
at all. We cannot judge the fairness of God by what we
get and what we don't get—or by what someone else
gets. He is not some cosmic Santa Claus or a giant Aspi-
rin, at the whim of mankind's caprice.

That day in my office, as Susan talked, I was reminded of
other women, disappointed because God didn't do as they
wanted, even denying that there was a God because of their
barren wombs. I was reminded also of a recent statement
by a Catholic bishop to the effect that in spite of all of man's
recent medical efforts in the area of making babies, a child
is still a gift from God. I was reminded above all of the
sovereignty of God in an era when it is becoming popular to
believe that matters of life and death are in the hands of
man rather than in the hands of God. God has remarkable
ways of showing us that in spite of all of our advances in
medical technology, He is still sovereign over the affairs of
mankind.

I was reminded, too, of a particular time in my own life,
in a completely different area, where God seemed far away
because He wasn't answering prayer in the way I wanted.
As I worked through that deep period in my life I wrote a
poem that expressed some of my feelings. It was a poem I
hadn't looked at in years. Yet recently, in the same month,
I have given it to Susan in my rejoicing with her, and at the
same time to another woman who is passing through a
deep valley over the death of a child and the desire for the
gift of another child.

When gently from my tight, clenched hands
God took of earthly things which I held dear,
Confused, his love I did not understand;
I grasped still more, lest more should disappear.

But yet in love he took until
To him alone I turned, for all else
Unsteady, apt to fade; reluctant, still
I gave to him the things I precious deemed.

He took, but then he gladly gave
First of himself, his love, his joy, and rest;
Until it seemed the things which I had saved
Were worthless toys compared to heaven's best.

Then, while with willing, open hands
I held all earthly gifts for him to see
And take or give, apart from my demands
He gave me back the things he took from me.[1]

For woman in particular, I believe, the maternal instinct
and the accompanying desire and talent to nurture are very
deep and instinctual. It is fashionable in some circles to say
that in this area there are no differences between men and
women. I do not agree, both from my own instinctual feelings as well as from those of my patients, both male and
female.

. . . The day when a woman enjoys her first love cuts her
in two. . . . The man is the same after his love as he was
before. The woman is from the day of her first love another.
That continues so all through life. The man spends a day by
a woman and goes away. His life and body are always the
same. The woman conceives. As a mother she is another
person than the woman without the child. She carries the
fruit of the night nine months long in her body. Something

grows. Something grows into her life that never again departs from it. She is a mother. She is and remains a mother even though her child die, though all her children die. For at one time she carried the child under her heart. And it does not go out of her heart ever again. Not even when it is dead. All this a man does not know.[2]

Because of woman's intense desire to bear children and nurture, the growth of medical technology in the area of alternate reproductive techniques is particularly confusing to her. While to many it offers the chance for a baby where there is no human possibility of having a child by natural means, for both the child and the parents the alternatives are sometimes a mixed blessing. Yet modern technology or not, God Himself is still ultimately in control in these at times frighteningly new aspects of the new-old attitude toward women and their bodies. He retains that right, and for many of us that knowledge provides a source of stability.

For while conception used to be a simple, private matter between two people, in many cases the bedroom has now been moved into the doctor's office or even the operating room and the laboratory. For some men and women who are both fertile but for one reason or another, such as a low sperm count, do not seem able to produce a child as readily as they wish to, artificial insemination has provided an answer. In artificial insemination, while the sperm is artificially introduced into the body, usually by a physician, fertilization still takes place within the woman's body. In contrast, with the use of *in vitro* or "in glass" fertilization, fertilization takes place outside the body in a glass and is then implanted into the womb, thus producing a so-called test-tube baby.

These relatively simple explanations are only the rudi-
mentary definitions of procedures that have a wide range of
possibilities, each containing within itself a new need for
clear thinking in the area of medical ethics. It is essential
that women become familiar with these procedures as they
become relevant to their own lives or that of their friends
and search for the biblical principles that apply to these
difficult issues.

In the area of artificial insemination, for example, I
know several Christian couples who have felt very comfortable morally and emotionally with the procedure and
other couples who have preferred to wait because they
fear that to go to, what are to them, such extreme measures to produce a child would amount to "forcing the
will of God." If one is to add a donor sperm to the procedure, where the sperm of someone other than the spouse
is introduced into the woman's body, many more couples
would object, feeling that the act, if not one of out-
and-out adultery, would amount to at least an adulterous
form of conception.

With in vitro fertilization the possibilities become much
more expansive, ranging from the fertilization of the sperm
and egg of a man and wife, where the wife has a defect in
the fallopian tubes, and then the implantation of that embryo back into the woman, to the use of a donor egg or
donor sperm or both. Where both egg and sperm are from
donors, the procedure results in something like adoption,
where the fertilized egg is adopted rather than the newborn
baby.

Because in vitro fertilization involves surgical procedures
that are expensive, it is economically prudent to fertilize
several eggs and thus produce several embryos. At this

point another ethical issue arises. What then is to be done with the unused embryos? Should the embryos be adopted out to couples who want to have children? Should they be used for research and then destroyed? Should they be used in the "farming" of organs, in essence grown in the laboratory for organ and tissue transplant? Or should they just be flushed down a drain?

Much research and experimentation is still needed for some of these possibilities, as well as others not mentioned here, to become possible, refined in their usage, and readily available to the public. But they have been and are being thought about and researched. We cannot hide our heads in horror and declare, "These things just can't be!" We cannot deny that the world we live in exists. But we can take measures to use what we can accept of this technology, and we can have a well-thought-out biblical basis for that which we cannot accept.

For even in less extreme examples of the use of in vitro fertilization, ethical questions arise faster than they are solved. To start with, our legal system is not equipped to handle these questions. For example, should the embryo be implanted in the womb of another woman who then acts as a surrogate mother for the genetic mother? This, it is argued, would be of advantage for those for whom pregnancy would be high risk or for those who just don't want to be bothered with nine months of pregnancy. What about the use of a donor egg? Again, is a donor egg tantamount to adultery? And to which mother does the resultant child belong?

Many of our ethical conclusions on the more extreme issues relating to in vitro fertilization will be based on our view of when life begins. Anthropologist Colin Turnbull comments:

> Most of us tend to think of our coming into being as coinciding with the miracle of birth. There are people, however, who see their beginning as taking place at least nine months earlier than that, even thinking of themselves in the most individual and material sense. In recounting their life history they do not start with "When I was born. . .," but rather with "When I was conceived. . . ."[3]

There is a biblical parallel to this way of thinking in Psalms 139:15, 16 (TLB): "You were there while I was being formed in utter seclusion! You saw me before I was born and scheduled each day of my life before I began to breathe. Every day was recorded in your Book!" If we view our lives as beginning at conception, we will have a difficult time with embryos washed down a drain or the use of fetuses for the farming of organs! If we do not believe that we start to be eternal beings at conception, then we will have to follow that belief to its logical conclusion and agree that what happens to these embryos and fetuses is of no consideration. Those who speak of treating these small beings "with consideration" or "respect" as they then destroy them, or worse, seem to me to exhibit the epitome of contradiction.

Moreover, with the kind of technical advances in medicine that we are observing today, it is absurd to believe there can be anything approaching an absolute sense of morality apart from a concrete belief in God. In the very informative book *Making Babies,* the authors suggest: ". . . Once we drop the idea that ethical knowledge is to be gained by special insight into the will of God, it ceases to be at all clear what is involved in being an expert in ethics. When it comes to ethical judgments, isn't anyone's opinion as good as anyone else's?"[4] We women who are Christians may have a hard time knowing the will of God in some of these less obvious areas of right and wrong, but at least we have a guidebook in the Bible and a Teacher in the indwelling Holy Spirit. We are not set loose like an anchorless ship on an uncharted, storm-tossed sea of confusion.

In March of 1984 the first frozen-embryo baby was born.

Loretta Leyland was, like many IVF patients, infertile because of diseased fallopian tubes. Her laparoscopy yielded ten eggs, an unusually large number. All the eggs were fertilized with sperm from her husband, and three were immediately transferred to Mrs. Leyland's womb. Of the remaining seven eggs, one was found to be developing abnormally and was discarded after examination. The remaining six were frozen in case no pregnancy resulted from the first transfer. This turned out to be the case, and so two months after the embryos had been frozen, they were thawed and examined once more. Three had survived the freezing process; these three were then transferred to Mrs. Leyland's womb. One implanted successfully and led to Zoe, a healthy, normal baby.[5]

A number of possibilities exist with freezing, among them the chance for a woman to have her children late in life without the risk of genetic defect that might normally exist at that time. However, as the choices pile up and women begin to choose so much about the genetic makeup, timing, and even method of conception of a child, natural frustrations arise. Already we have a tendency toward mechanized sex for those people who carefully time intercourse in order to produce a pregnancy. To be able to freeze a fetus and thus choose even the long-range timing of the baby's birth can produce considerable feelings of anxiety. To quote psychologist Dr. Rollo May as he comments about the issue from the point of view of just simple birth control alone:

There is also the dilemma of personal responsibility which comes from the freedom to choose to have a baby or not. It has been possible to plan for babies for the last four decades, and though we have acted upon that power, we have never accepted the psychological personal responsibility for it. Our blithe evasion of that issue comes out in the guilt we feel as a whole society toward our children. We do everything for them, we cater to their development and their whims, we count it a sign of our broadmindedness and virtue that we give in to them on every moral issue (and now on marijuana) so that the poor children have an impossible time trying to find something about these always-giving-in parents against which they can revolt. When they go away, we say, "Have a good time," and we get worried if they don't have a good time and worried if they have too good a time. And all the while we are secretly envious of them and their youth and resentful of how good they have had it as compared with how hard we had it. Through all of this treating our young like little royalty, heirs apparent to heaven knows what, we are the maids-in-waiting, chauffeurs, cooks, nurses, bottomless money bags, home teachers, camp leaders—until it is no wonder our children stand up and scream, "For heaven's sake, leave us *alone!*" And that is the biggest threat of all to us—for we are filled with some nameless, pervasive guilt about our children and can't let go. And the guilt we are expiating is not about some specific thing we did or didn't do in rearing them; it is about the basic fact of having children in the first place. For no longer does "God" decide we are to have children; we do.

And who has even begun to comprehend the meaning of that tremendous fact?[6]

In contrast to the calculatedness and at times coldness of our modern technology and its influence on having babies, once again Colin Turnbull discusses what he calls the "art of becoming as it is practiced by the Mbuti hunter-gatherers still living in the Ituri Forest of northeastern Zaire."[7] In describing the behavior of the pregnant woman in this part of the world, Turnbull continues:

As the pregnancy continues, the mother-to-be pursues her normal everyday life without much change right up to the moment of delivery, but she increasingly avoids activities or situations that might tax her physically or emotionally. She adorns her body with leaves and flowers, perhaps in readiness. . . . In the last few months she takes to going off on her own, to her favorite spot in the forest, and singing to the child in her womb.

The lullaby that she sings is special in several ways. It is the only form of song that can be sung as a solo and it is composed by the mother for that particular child within her womb. It is sung for no other, it is sung by no other. The young mother sings it quietly, reassuringly, rocking herself, sometimes with her hands on her belly, or gently splashing her hands or feet in the water of her favorite stream or river, or rustling them through leaves, or warming herself at a fire. In a similar way she talks to the child, according it the intelligence, though not the knowledge of an adult. There is no baby talk. What she says to the child is clear, informative, reassuring, and comforting. She tells it of the forest world into which it will soon emerge, repeating simple phrases such as those perhaps already "heard" by the unborn baby while its mother was off on the hunt: the forest is good, the forest is kind; mother forest, father forest.

Some mothers describe the place where the child will be born, the other children it will meet and play with. . . . And once the children are born and begin to learn to speak they hear these stories over and over again and it all becomes so familiar that it is as if they were conscious of being conceived at that place and that time of day. . . . Mbuti see their life as beginning the moment they were wanted for that is when they were conceived. . . .[8]

Concludes Turnbull,

In one sense it is not of the slightest importance that the unborn child can hardly be expected to understand what is being said to it. Nor does it matter whether or not the emotional content of what the mother is thinking and doing and saying is in any way transferred to the unborn baby's consciousness. It is enough that the mother, at least, is reinforcing her own concept of the world . . . giving herself confidence [in her world]. That confidence alone would be an auspicious beginning to any life.[9]

In Zaire, that confidence that is felt by the expectant mother as she talks to her yet unborn child is only the beginning of many years of nurturing.

Regardless of how or where a life is conceived, there seems to me to be an unwritten law of nature that makes the mother the initial and primary nurturer of the child. It is an instinct felt before the child's birth and often even before its conception. Once the child is born, the father, other relatives, and friends, and eventually the more professional world of teachers, tutors, and the like are added to this number. But at first, however brief and unsatisfactory the encounter, even if the child dies or is given up for adoption, it is the mother and her child alone. No wonder deep emotional and spiritual roots start in every human being with that fundamental nurturing influence of woman as mother. It is no wonder that throughout all of our lives that influence remains.

According to Webster the word *nurture* involves concepts of nourishing, training, and upbringing. It means "to further the development of." In a more precise definition Webster explains that nurturing involves "the sum of the influences modifying the expression of the genetic potentialities of an organism."

As it accompanies and at times motivates the maternal desire for children, the nurturing of children and of people in general seems to be a particularly innate desire within woman. Some would deny this urge in order to insure equality of women with men or to argue the efficacy of male parenting. To me equality has nothing to do with this issue. Once again, men and women are definitely equal in worth. But they are also very different in kind. And one of the inborn capabilities of a woman is to nurture.

In all our striving for women's rights, it seems to me that the desire to nurture has been one of the needs of a woman and indeed one of her God-given talents that has been neglected. Now several generations of children have grown up knowing little of what it means to be nurtured by their mothers. Many women who feel that by having a baby they are fulfilling a need do not complete that fulfillment by going on to nurture that child. Then they wonder why childbearing is not as satisfying as they thought it would be. Getting pregnant and bearing a healthy child is only the beginning, not the end, of having children.

In his short book *A Christmas Memory*, the late Truman Capote described his relationship with an older cousin who appeared to have been the chief source of any nurturing he received before, at about ten years of age, he was shipped off to boarding schools. This cousin was a simple woman of about sixty years of age. Said Mr. Capote:

> My friend has never been to a picture show, nor does she intend to: "I'd rather hear you tell the story, Buddy [her pet name for him]. That way I can imagine it more. Besides a person my age shouldn't squander their eyes. When the Lord comes, let me see him clear." In addition to never having seen a movie, she has never: eaten in a restaurant, traveled more than five miles from home, received or sent a telegram, read anything except funny papers and the Bible, worn cosmetics, cursed, wished someone harm, told a lie on purpose, let a hungry dog go hungry. Here are a few things she has done, does do: killed with a hoe the biggest rattle-snake ever seen in the county (sixteen rattles), dip snuff (secretly), tame hummingbirds (just try it) till they balance on her finger, tell ghost stories (we both believe in ghosts) so tingling they chill you in July, talk to herself, take walks in the rain, grow the prettiest japonicas in town, know the recipe for every sort of old-time Indian cure, including a magical wart-remover.[10]

A Christmas Memory is based on the yearly ritual that "Buddy" and his friend performed each November, when the weather reminded them of the oncoming Christmas season and the two of them collected the ingredients for, and then made and distributed, a large number of very special fruitcakes. For Mr. Capote the experience was

one of the highlights of his childhood, and his relationship with his cousin seems to be almost the only encounter with nurturing he was allowed in those short years
before, as he so poignantly put it: "Life separates us.
Those Who Know Best decide that I belong in a military
school. And so follows a miserable succession of bugle-
blowing prisons, grim reveille-ridden summer camps. I
have a new home too. But it doesn't count. Home is
where my friend is, and there I never go."[11] Such is the
essence of nurturing. It does not require brilliance or
money or sophistication; but children need a great deal of
it if they are to grow up whole.

In my own childhood I remember things like going to a
children's concert to hear *Peter and the Wolf* and the accompanying explanations from my parents about the various instruments involved. I remember cutting out
Christmas cookies and learning the do's and don'ts of baking from my mother, who was an excellent cook. I remember countless stories from my mother's childhood and from
books she herself had treasured as a child. I remember
sewing lessons, knitting lessons, and crocheting lessons. I
remember special times, like shopping for clothes and then
having lunch in a tearoom where I was the only child. I
remember discussions about truthfulness and kindness
and, above all, about God. Other women also shared in my
nurturing. As an example, one aunt taught me Chinese
cooking and Chinese lettering before I could even write in
English. My next-door neighbor's mother taught me em-
broidery.

True, I also learned from my father, things like how to
nail a board and how to fish. Later in life my father as
well as my uncle were sources of endless intellectual discussions on every topic from literature and life in Swe-

den, where my father was born, to theology, which was
the forte of my uncle. These discussions, too, were nurturing, and they never stopped until the day each of them
died. I miss that support tremendously, even now. But in
those early days of childhood I was nurtured most from
the countless little things my mother and other women
did with me. Then I needed, and every child alive today
needs, the special nurturing for which women are particularly equipped.

Yet just as nurturing is not exclusively the province of
women, childhood is not the only time when we need
nurturing. Within a marriage and within the family in
general it is needed, and more often than not the woman is
the center of nurturing. Yet the truly cohesive family requires a certain mutuality of nurturing between husband
and wife. In 1 Corinthians 11:11, 12 (AMPLIFIED) Paul says:
"Nevertheless, in [the plan of] the Lord and from His point
of view woman is not apart from and independent of man,
nor is man aloof from and independent of woman; For as
woman was made from man, even so man is also born of
woman. And all [whether male or female go forth] from
God (as their Author)."

There is, furthermore, a complementary function of the
husband to that of the role of the wife. Reading on in
Ephesians 5:25 (PHILLIPS), Paul says: "The husband must
give his wife the same sort of love that Christ gave to the
Church, when he sacrificed himself for her." For while the
woman may be the major source of nurturing in a family,
she should not be the *only* source, and she in turn must
receive nurturing back, or she will run dry in her ability to
give.

Part of any mutual nurturing within a marriage requires hearing what the marriage partner is saying re-

garding his or her needs. Not long ago in my office a man said of his wife, "I love her." Five minutes later his wife said to me, "If John would only say he loved me." A week later the wife said to her husband in my presence, "I wish I had some time to be alone." Just a few minutes later John countered with, "I'd like to have the time to go bowling, but Barbara wants me with her all the time." As they talked, each time they tuned each other out I stopped them and forced them to really listen. Up to this time each of them had focused more on his or her own viewpoint and how to express it than on what the other one was saying.

After a few sessions they understood some needs the other had in a way that had never occurred to them before. Sometimes in a marriage two people become frustrated just because they never stop long enough to really hear what the other one is saying. What is true between a husband and wife is also true between a parent and a child or two friends. For without truly hearing where someone is coming from, any attempts at nurturing and building up or even comforting are rendered at least partially ineffective.

While I believe that nurturing is peculiarly instinctive to a woman with her child, all of us should indeed be encouraged and taught to once again revive the sometimes lost art of nurturing one another.

On the night of the car accident that ultimately took my mother's life, I came home from the hospital emergency room somewhere around midnight. I had forgotten that I had a dog at home who needed feeding and walking, and I myself certainly hadn't eaten. I was upset, tired, and almost passive about doing anything immediate to meet my own needs. My mind was still back in that hospital emergency room. As a friend and I approached my apartment, I saw that my light was on. I felt faintly cheered by the sight. A woman who managed the building had come in, walked and fed my dog, Thackeray, put the lights on, and was now there to see that I ate and to listen if I wanted to talk. I was down and vulnerable. I particularly needed nurturing, and those small acts of kindness will be long remembered.

For nurturing on any level is not necessarily complicated. It can be the cool touch of a kind nurse on a fevered brow; the enjoyment of an afternoon cup of tea with a friend, in the middle of a busy day; a note, a card, a telephone call. We can offer nurturing in something as important as encouragement regarding a disappointing child or as mundane as instruction regarding the use of a new appliance. Indeed, particularly on the adult level, nurturing has a curious resemblance to the many biblical instructions to encourage one another or to the definition of the Body of Christ, where each part needs what the other part has to contribute to the whole.

In a day of computerized living, where phone machines answer phone machines and dialing multiple sets of numbers on a phone in response to the taped message of a telephone operator replaces the need for direct contact between the caller and that operator, we can easily forget we are still vulnerable human beings in need of the nurturing that only comes through a human touch. Particularly in the area of the family, where people are together less because everyone, including the children, is perhaps too busy, personal encounters and the gift of time cannot be replaced by videogames and expensive gadgets. Above all, babies may be easier to come by now, with all the advances in medical technology, but once they are here, they require the same things they have always required: love and the nurturing of a mother who takes the time to raise them. Only then can we in all honesty offer the words of the old Watts cradle hymn:

Mayest thou live to know and fear Him,
Trust and love Him all thy days,
Then go dwell forever near Him,
See His face and sing His praise.

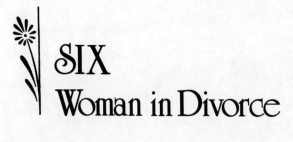

SIX
Woman in Divorce

Awoman in her mid thirties sat across from me in my counseling office and posed her question: "Do I have a biblical basis for this divorce I am seeking?"

Jan and her husband, Rick, were both Christians, but during the past two years a great change had taken place within Rick and consequently in his relationship with Jan. As Jan put it, "Each day Rick resembles less and less the man whom I originally married. That Rick was kind and considerate; this Rick is argumentative and hostile." The incident that precluded Jan's entertaining further thoughts about preserving the marriage had occurred two days before she picked up the phone and made an appointment with me. In a fit of rage because his four-year-old daughter had spilled her milk at the dinner table, Rick had picked up a knife and, waving it wildly, had chased the child to her room.

Nor had Rick's fits of irrationality been limited to that one occasion. In the evening after dinner he frequently became drunk and would play with his loaded gun, not caring that three children under ten were playing in the same room.

Psychologically, too, Rick was destructive to his family. He would look at his six-year-old daughter and say things like, "You're ugly," or when she tripped and fell, "How come you can't be more like other kids your age?" Jan also came in for her share of his verbal abuse, which had almost destroyed her sense of good self-esteem. Even more Jan feared the effect he was having on their three small children during their formative years, when children develop their basic self-image. After only a year of this abuse, the children were having nightmares; they were excessively shy in social situations and were performing poorly in school. Above all, Jan feared what Rick might do someday in a real act of violence.

Jan had tried everything, from applying spiritual principles to her marriage to psychological counseling. County authorities had been notified of the potential danger to the children, so periodically the children had been removed from the home, each time until Rick seemed better. But every time he improved, it was only briefly so that, as he put it later, he could get his kids back from those "nosy social workers." Apart from meeting the minimum requirements of the county in order to regain his children, Rick refused any help with his problems. Indeed he seemed unwilling to even admit he had problems.

At this point Jan was questioning her ability to stay on in this situation, which threatened the physical well-being of both her and her children. Yet Rick had always been faithful to her sexually. She could not in all honesty fulfill her church's prerequisite for divorce: adultery. At times she had found herself praying that he would be unfaithful so that she could be free of him with a clear conscience before God. When she was particularly desperate, she wished him dead. Then she felt ashamed of her prayers.

Everyone she had talked to at her church had a different viewpoint, ranging from, "Stay with him and leave it in God's hands," to, "since there is no sexual immorality involved, you don't have a scriptural basis for divorce." Then some would ambiguously add: "This must be an exception, somehow. You obviously can't go on living with him." None of these viewpoints were very helpful.

Jan seemed to be facing a dilemma that gave her no way out. Any answer seemed wrong: It could not be right to take chances with her own life and the lives of her children; yet from the viewpoint of her church, divorce was wrong for her. The most compassionate of her friends were essentially telling her that she should go ahead and sin by getting a divorce in order to secure her family's safety. Was it impossible, therefore, to guarantee her children's safety and at the same time please God? Would He who commanded His disciples to let the little children come to Him not be the first to want to protect these children whom He had entrusted to her care?

Talking about a woman's role in handling a divorce emotionally and in helping her children to adjust to the changes is relatively easy. It is far harder for a woman to handle divorce as she deals with the rightness or wrongness of that divorce.

Matthew 5:32 offers the most concise statement on divorce given by Christ in the Gospels. "But I tell you that every man who puts away his wife except on the ground of unfaithfulness causes her to commit adultery, and whoever marries her when so divorced commits adultery" (WEYMOUTH).

"Unfaithfulness" here is translated as "unchastity" in the Moffatt translation and, with less accuracy, "fornication" in the King James Version. In the Greek the meaning of the word "fornication" (*porneia*) goes beyond adultery to include any immoral sexual act. "It was used of sexual sin as a whole, and also of specific sexual sins. The context in which it appears determines the sense to be assigned to it. It follows that from the 4th century B.C. in Greece and 200 B.C. among Greek-speaking Jews down to 96 A.D., porneia and its cognates were used not only of fornication but of practically every other specific sin, as well as of all sexual sins taken collectively."[1] Such reputable biblical scholars as Augustine, Clement, Strong, Rotherham, Vincent, Wuest, Goodspeed, Douay, Wesley, Ascott, and others concur with such an interpretation of the word *porneia*. Presumably the sins included in the meaning of this word could timelessly include incest, adultery, child molestation, homosexuality, sadism, and other sexual acts defined as immoral by scriptural precept, not just by what is considered acceptable in a given society at a given time.

While the specifics of modesty, for example, may vary from culture to culture and decade to decade, actual sexual mores are quite clearly set forth in the Scriptures and do not change. There was a time when exposing one's "limbs" was considered immodest for a woman in this country. Now most Christian women feel quite comfortable wearing shorts, or dresses and skirts that fall well above ankle length. Short hair, tank-type bathing suits, lipstick, and hair dye were all considered to be at least on the borderline of immodesty a few years back. Yet today most Christians find all these accoutrements of female style acceptable. In contrast, such sexual acts as adultery and incest, while they may occur more frequently, within the church as well as without, are still considered immoral by most Christians and by biblical teaching.

However, the real question Christ answers in the book of Matthew is whether or not a man should be able to divorce a woman "for every cause." According to the Jewish law of the time, a man could get a divorce for almost any reason. When the question was asked of Christ, ". . . Is it lawful for a man to put away his wife for every cause?" (Matthew 19:3), the Pharisees were probably trying to trap Christ. It was not an honest question asked by those who were seeking truth.

Even the rabbis of that day, representing the religious establishment, disagreed on the appropriate grounds for divorce. At one extreme, one school of interpretation allowed divorce for such a trivial act as a burned supper! Contrary to the basic Jewish ideal, marriage under these conditions was often a mockery. In one case recorded by Alfred Edersheim, two rabbis decided to each marry a woman for a day and then divorce her.

Women were the real victims of the looseness of the Jewish laws. Under Jewish law a woman could not divorce a man on her own. Furthermore, because the culture did not provide much opportunity for women who wished to support themselves, women who were divorced by their husbands were in danger of being thrown out on the street and left in a helpless position. The situation was therefore quite different from our culture today, and the real women's-rights issues were centered around the protection afforded women by strict divorce laws. As a rule, women in the first century A.D. Jewish culture had little to gain and everything to lose by a divorce.

In contrast, the Greek and Roman cultures of the same

era allowed women to obtain legal divorces for themselves. In reality, however, the liberalization of divorce effected little change in the life of the average woman; for economically a woman still would have had a hard time supporting herself without a husband. Perhaps the harsh economic realities account for the high incidence of prostitution at that time, for that was one way in which a woman *could* support herself.

While righteousness rather than the alleviation of human suffering was Christ's primary concern in the matter of divorce, the practical effect of His rather strict pronouncement on divorce was that of protecting women from the harshness of the economic results of divorce in the culture of His time. Thus protection rather than denial of the rights of women was the practical outcome of Christ's teaching on divorce.

Yet clear-cut as Christ's teaching on divorce seems to be from a biblical point of view, for a situation such as that of Jan's marriage, the issues still seem unclear and complicated. In Jan's marriage there had been no outward act of sexual infidelity, so one must search further.

In 1 Corinthians 7 we have Paul's commentary on a situation that had arisen within the newly established church, which was not covered by any of the words of Christ in the Gospels: that of what to do with an unbelieving spouse. Only after Christ's ascension into heaven could this have become an issue, for with the coming of the Holy Spirit the church was established. Says the Apostle: "And unto the married I command, yet not I, but the Lord, Let not the wife depart from her husband: But and if she depart, let her remain unmarried, or be reconciled to her husband: and let not the husband put away his wife" (vv. 10, 11). Then Paul continues with the exception: "But if the unbelieving depart, let him depart. A brother or a sister is not under bondage in such cases: but God hath called us to peace" (v. 15).

At this point in the study of those Scriptures relating to divorce one must confront the issue of remarriage as it relates to divorce. For when Christ speaks of causing a woman to commit adultery by seeking a divorce that does not have a biblical basis, it is clearly in the remarriage that the adulterous act is committed. In the cultural context of His remarks, it was to be expected that the man would seek the divorce with the woman, and because of her economic straits she would feel compelled to remarry.

In his excellent book *Divorce and Remarriage*, Guy Duty says: "In this case of Matthew 5:32 our Lord shows that the man who divorces his wife for any cause except fornication causes her to commit adultery in remarriage. The Lord assumed that the woman would remarry. The reason she commits adultery is that she becomes involved in sexual sin with another man while still the wife of the man who divorced her. The divorce did not dissolve the marriage."[2] In the verses in 1 Corinthians, where the believing spouse is told not to leave the unbeliever, she is told to stay single if she does leave him; for such a reason is not seen in the Scriptures as a valid basis for divorce. Once again divorce was not to be granted "for every cause."

In the day in which we live, we, too, are increasingly under the rule of divorce "for every cause." To think consistently with biblical principles and teaching, we must conclude that when Christians divorce and remarry at caprice, before God they are choosing to live in adultery, and indeed sometimes in a string of single acts of polygamy.

Yet biblically based divorce seems to completely free the person involved for remarriage, for while God is above all a

God of purity, He is also not a God of bondage. In the Greek the word for divorce is *apoluo*. Its Old Testament equivalent is *kerithuth*. Both words carry with them the concept of a complete cut, a total dissolution. "The primary meaning of the Greek 'apolou' is 'to set free.' "[3] To quote Guy Duty again:

> After such a divorce, the marriage is null, void, and dead. It is the same as if the adulterous mate had died. If dissolution can be proved, then there is no question about the right to remarriage, because our opponents deny remarriage on the grounds of non-dissolution.
>
> A dissolution-divorce was the only kind of divorce known to the Jews, and Jesus did not give the faintest hint of anything else. It was also the only kind of divorce known to the Greeks and Romans. The separation-divorce was not invented by Latin monks until several centuries after Christ.[4]

Even in those verses in 1 Corinthians that speak of the unbelieving spouse who leaves, many scholars agree that the right to remarry is implied. According to Theodore Woolsey: "The Protestant commentators of the 16th and 17th centuries, or the large number of them, draw the liberty of remarriage after desertion from the word of Paul, 1 Corinthians 7:15."[5] Woolsey also quotes Grotius as translating 1 Corinthians 7:15: "She is not bound to remain unmarried and to wait or to seek for reconciliation." Bishop Lightfoot adds weight to this interpretation by stating: "The Christian is not so enslaved by such an alliance that he or she may not be set free."[6] And Matthew Henry concurs, "The deserted party seems to be left more at liberty . . . to marry another person. It does not seem reasonable that they should still be bound. . . . In such a case marriage would be servitude indeed."[7]

Thus in the verses in 1 Corinthians we not only have considerable consistency with other Scriptures on the right to remarry in situations where divorce has a specific biblical basis, we also have a situation arising in this newly established church, which is then dealt with, using biblical principles. God's justice is maintained, yet it includes an additional principle of freedom from dissension and bondage.

In the example of Jan's marriage, we have a situation not directly dealt with in the Scriptures, in which we must use good sense, based on both biblical precept and biblical principles. Psychiatrist Viktor Frankl described his conflicting emotions as he and his wife faced internment and possible death by the Nazis. He asked his wife to make him one promise, that if she was confronted with the choice of having sex with someone else or execution that she would choose to submit herself sexually. For, reasons Frankl, to choose death for oneself is a greater wrong than adultery. The only possible choice in such a situation is to choose the lesser of the two evils.

From one point of view, Jan's dilemma is similar. She is wrong in allowing herself and her children to be destroyed, yet, according to many, she is wrong if she leaves this man. In such a situation she might have to make a decision in terms of what seems most right, or, as the late Walter Trobisch would say, do what is most loving.

Remember too, that, like Jan, not every person seeking divorce does so on the basis of "incompatibility" or because he or she has outgrown a spouse. Not every person who seeks a divorce is trying to take the easy way out. Sometimes they take the only sane way out. In my work with families I have encountered situations ranging from the problems that face two people who are growing in two different directions, to families ravaged by the drug abuse of a teenager, to families where the pathology extended itself to murder and even cannibalism. Such encounters give me a healthy respect for the validity of the theology of the fall of man!

I have also felt disillusionment, at times, when I have sat in one counseling session and heard about a string of sexual affairs, engaged in over the years by a member of the pastoral staff of a sound, Bible-believing church, and two hours later heard from one of the parishioners of the same church that she is afraid to leave a marriage that threatens her very life, because the pastor whom I had just seen might "be disappointed in her." Nor has this been a single, isolated incident in my experience. For although it is certainly not the norm, it has happened more than once.

Yet if we're talking about *your* life, and not the person next door, even outgrowing someone can be painful enough to at least make you feel you want out! If I have learned one thing from my years of counseling, it has been that it is easy to be inflexible about issues until they become *your* issues. Good children from good Christian homes don't go wrong—until *your* children do. Marriages centered around Christ don't disintegrate—until suddenly the cracks appear in *your* marriage. Suddenly a person who might otherwise have been deeply opposed to divorce begins to try to find that scriptural "out" that will make divorce a little more accessible to him or her, now that he or she no longer talks about *someone else's* life.

This chapter does not aim to establish principles of behavior that outdo God in their strictness or to find an "out" for someone who has newly discovered his or her humanity. Rather it establishes some general biblical principles that will hold true for our own lives and the lives of those we counsel. For we face a danger: Extremism breeds extremism. If I establish legalistic rather than biblical laws for my life, then someday, when I undergo emotional pressures that are too much for me, I may well turn and go to the other extreme and deny not only the legalism but biblical truth itself. I see Bible teachers who have literally clubbed people with do's and don'ts suddenly leave their wives and children and go off with a younger woman. The wife typically ends up in my office, saying something like: "I don't understand how this could have happened. Tom was such a devout man." Tom may not have been such a devout man as he was a legalistic man. When the house fell, it fell hard, for there were no foundations!

I hear the popular explanation that some kind of mid-life crisis causes such an occurrence. To a degree that may be true. But in many cases I think "mid-life crisis" can be a cop-out for a lack of balance and spiritual depth that may have been missing from a life for many years.

Along somewhat different lines, if we take the Bible as a book of principles, then view the scriptural stance on divorce within the cultural context of that time, we arrive at a perspective some may find helpful. Taking biblical truth within a cultural perspective does not mean we rationalize away the Bible when we don't like what it says. Nor does it take away from a literal interpretation of a Book that is literally inspired. However, for example, when Paul commands a woman to have her head covered in the local church meeting, the basic principle is that of appearing moral. Prostitutes went out with their heads uncovered, not women with morals. Therefore the principle is to both be and appear to be moral. We as Christians are commanded to give no appearance of evil. The application of the principle for that day was for women to wear a head covering. Today, apart from the Catholic Church and smaller groups such as the Plymouth Brethren, most Christians agree that women can worship in God's house without hats. Hats in our culture are more a sign of style or even vanity than of any particular godliness. Yet even now, while I do not feel that they are mandatory, when a woman wears a hat out of a desire to please God and to fulfill the Scriptures, I am sure He honors that motive.

In a similar way in connection with divorce, God stresses the principle of the sanctity of marriage. He does not approve of divorce "for every cause." The Pharisees would have liked to trap Christ Himself into approval of such laxness. The oneness epitomized in the sexual union is the image used in connection with Christ and the church. This principle was applied to the Jewish-Greek-Roman world as giving grounds for divorce on the basis of sexual immorality only.

Yet in a culture like ours, where women are fully able to support themselves and social and legal institutions protect the rights of women and children, perhaps we can make a different application of certain Scriptures, as long as we adhere to Christ's principle of the extreme sanctity of marriage. Perhaps in such a social setting, where women's rights are no longer a survival issue, a divorce or even a legal separation might be the right move for a Christian who finds his or her marriage remaining deeply and permanently destructive, though much time, effort and professional counseling have been put into making the marriage work. A relationship such as that of Jan and her husband would certainly seem to destroy the meaning of any sexual union as completely as any act of sexual immorality and could be considered a form of desertion as complete as the actual physical desertion of an unbelieving husband. Indeed hate and destructiveness would seem to make such a union a mockery. For it is indeed possible to turn sexual activity into something far from sacred.

I once heard a young woman say that once two people had sex, they were married in the eyes of God. I have wondered since if she would feel the same way about rape—or incest! I have seen a five-year-old who was brutally molested by her so-called Christian father, who damaged her so badly and so calculatedly that he first used alcohol as an anesthetic. Yet the pastor who advised the mother to divorce the husband refused to perform the ceremony for her second marriage, this time to a stable, godly man! I have talked to a ten-year-old who was repeatedly awakened from a deep sleep by her father's act of sodomy. I have known of women raped in their own marriage beds by husbands who had promised to love and protect them. I have also seen many people, male and female alike, to whom the sex act is a sort of self-indulgent, competitive sport focused on new techniques and the stimulation of videotapes. The sex act is not always a sacred one, but it is certainly meant to be.

Biblical interpretation in the area of divorce is not easy or always clear, as evidenced by the number of reputable biblical scholars who disagree with one another. Certainly one must be exceedingly careful in adding cultural considerations to biblical interpretation, especially regarding a subject that the Bible talks about as seriously as it does divorce and adultery (the latter was punishable by death under Old Testament law). It is a dangerous thing to *add* to the Word of God, yet at the same time we are all obligated to *interpret* the Scriptures to the individual circumstances of our lives. In this quest James 1 promises us wisdom if we ask in faith, and each of us ultimately must take that wisdom in application to our own consciences as we counsel the women who seek our help.

We have looked at the role woman has played historically in the matter of divorce and how that role might affect the moral grounds for divorce or legal separation in our own age. But equally important as the role woman plays in the grounds for divorce is the one she plays when that divorce actually takes place.

Following a divorce the various roles that any one woman plays may change drastically, probably more dramatically for the woman than for the man. Many evangelical churches today still emphasize that a woman should not go to work, but should stay home. For a woman from this background to suddenly be shunted into the marketplace, where perhaps she does not even want to be, can be a threatening change of life-style. Mothers suddenly find that for at least five days out of seven they are now both mother and father. Broken plumbing and overdue bills may become their tasks for the first time. One woman found calling a doctor for her sick child an almost traumatic experience. "Do I dare call him without first calling my husband?" she said to me.

At the same time that women's roles have expanded, so to speak, social supports may decrease as mutual friends try to remain neutral and as social occasions geared toward couples do not suddenly change to accommodate those newly divorced. Singles' groups for those who are now separated from their spouses may be filled with "losers" or those "on the make" sexually, and even the local church suddenly may appear to be more couple oriented than it seemed before. Anchors are lost, and changing roles are inevitable.

For most women who get divorces or legal separations, the biggest role change is that they must go out and get a job in order to support themselves. While at this time a woman may need to develop her social life, by necessity she finds the bulk of her time taken up in the marketplace. For an untrained woman in particular this is a difficult prospect. She may discover that she can only get a low-paying, boring job, where her work status is equal to that of a recent high-school graduate. Or, worse still, she may become the victim of age discrimination. First she may have lost her marriage to a younger woman; now she may feel that even her job is in jeopardy, because she is too old. Women who never felt old in their lives may feel as if they aged overnight.

For a woman who finds herself in this position, additional job training may help, and perhaps the advice of good friends will provide answers for some of the practical problems that arise in the home. In this area the Body of Christ should function, for the local church has a responsibility to those who are helpless in its midst. The Bible cites widows and orphans, but the newly bereaved or divorced, those without natural families, those located far from their families, such as students, and others who are temporarily helpless or at least vulnerable are to be the church's special object of comfort and assistance.

Prevention, however, is perhaps one of the best cures. A woman always needs training in some marketable skill. No husband should so shelter his wife that she can't handle money and make intelligent decisions regarding such issues as insurance, house payments, and taxes. Certainly one should not anticipate divorce, but widows face these same problems. Out of every two people in a marriage, one will be single as a result of the spouse's death. More often than not that one person is the wife. In the emotional upheaval of a divorce or death a woman feels more comfortable if she can already drive, handle the business of the home, and if necessary go out and get a job.

Even roles that are commonly thought of as female change in their scope during a divorce. The most outstanding change in this category is raising children, whether or not the woman becomes the custodial parent. If a woman has to work, she will spend less time with her children and may feel guilty about that. This guilt becomes particularly unfair if a male-dominated clergy teaches her that her place is in the home, while her husband, who in spite of the fact that he supported that church view, now blithely goes off into the sunset with his new love. Whatever the reason for her guilt (for indeed the woman, too, may be the offender in the marriage and may neglect her children for another man), it may cause her to spend excessive amounts of money on her children "to make up for what they're going through."

Regarding the "quality of time" idea, much criticism has been offered to women who work. It has been rightly argued that some women use the notion "the quality, not the quantity, of time you spend with a child counts" as an excuse to do their own thing and neglect their children. Having acknowledged that possibility, let's realize that many women do not have a choice about how much time they spend with their children.

Moreover, I know of any number of women who, while they are home all the time, rarely do anything of value for or with their children. Many women who work spend smaller yet more valuable portions of time nurturing their children. From an overall perspective, whether she is married or single, a woman who works outside the home, has a good social life, and spends time with her children, doing things which they all enjoy, is more effective than the guilt-ridden mother who spends all her time with them but feels resentful and unhappy.

It goes without saying that the woman who not only stays home with her children but also *wants* to will exert a positive influence on those children. If this is not her attitude, however, the children will probably do better if their mother is out of the home some of the time and then fulfilled and contented when she is home with them.

Whatever the role changes that occur because of divorce and regardless of whose fault it is, loneliness is probably the outstanding emotional outgrowth. While both the husband and the wife probably feel lonely, the woman may experience it on a deeper level, especially if she has been in a dependent role. Sleeping alone, eating alone, and waking up in the middle of the night to find no one there all can be deeply painful experiences for a woman who has never really been alone before. As one woman put it: "I used to wake up and reach out to touch him, and he wasn't there."

When a woman feels guilt and rejection in the middle of loneliness, the pain becomes even more acute. There is often guilt over whether more could have been done to save the marriage. Unfortunately, too often those who did little to save a marriage feel the least guilty, and those who struggled hard to make it work now tend to think perhaps they could have worked a little harder after all. Feelings of rejection, too, gnaw away at many as they feel that if somehow they had been better persons this wouldn't have happened. Women who are busy at home with children seem particularly vulnerable to this feeling of inadequacy, especially if their husbands have gone off with other women, "out of the blue," so to speak.

Many women in divorce wonder if they have lost their attractiveness. A middle-aged, older woman may be more prone to this fear, since for her childbearing is no longer possible, menopause is at hand, and her very feeling of femininity may feel threatened. At the same time her male counterpart may go out with younger women in order to boost his male ego. However he will in general tend to be less vulnerable to growing old, since for him age may merely mean graying hair that will make him look more distinguished than old.

Professional counseling often helps a woman involved in a divorce, and it should not be shunned as though it implied failure, either spiritually or psychologically. But apart from or in addition to counseling, very simple, practical things may help.

Any divorce produces and precipitates a myriad of psychological tapes. The regrets of the past and the "what ifs" of the future can torture an already distraught mind. "Why didn't I pay more attention to how I looked, now that I see him with that new, young woman?" "What if I can't support myself and the children, especially if he takes off and neglects his child support?" "Why did God let this happen? Doesn't He love me anymore?" "I can't make it alone; I just can't go on. . . ."

Then there are the tapes of memory: "that first time we met . . ." or "the first kiss," "the first time we made love," "the first baby," "the first house." There may be bitterness: "After all I've done for him . . ."; "I've given him the best years of my life."

The answer to dealing with these old tapes is not analysis, not even, in general, "getting it all out." At this point counseling can actually hinder a woman's progress, if the sessions center around dredging up the past and commiserating about the future. The key to getting beyond all the emotional chaos lies in knowing that one can have power over one's emotions and then acting on that knowledge, cutting the tapes. We live in a time when it is popular to feel that one has little control over one's emotions. "It's just the way I am" has become a favorite cop-out, as though I could never change the "way I am." Even our morality is tinged with this bondage to feelings: If it feels good it's right. In truth our feelings form very unreliable gauges of morality, and "letting it all hang out" can be a very painful way to go through life. We can cut old tapes by a simple act of the will. It may take practice to make it work, since we formed a habit of running the old tapes, much to our own distress and that of those around us.

Cutting old tapes does not mean we should go to an extreme and never talk about our feelings. To do so would be to go back a hundred years and unlearn all the positive things about the human personality we have discovered from the study of human emotions. Cutting tapes means we don't dwell on these negative feelings and occurrences of the past; rather we simply cut them and go on. For me cutting tapes carries with it the image of turning off a tape recorder. A patient of mine had another image: that of literally cutting a piece of tape with a pair of scissors. Once when she had a bad week, she came into my office and said: "My scissors broke this week." Still used to her life-long pattern of playing old tapes, like the rest of us, at times she found the very simplicity of just cutting the old tapes difficult.

After one has cut the tapes, however, she must refocus, or those old tapes will come back like a flood. To *focus* means to act as well as to think in a positive direction. One woman going through a divorce found herself first staying at home, then in bed. Such a simple task as going to the grocery store was agony, but she had to make that effort if she wanted to pull herself out of her depression. She cut the old, despairing tapes and got out of bed. With the help of some professional counseling, she became a whole person once again. Another woman developed some talent in art, which had lain dormant for years but now became an absorbing hobby. Art was a focus for her, and it made her less vulnerable to the old tapes. Still another woman began going to a weekly Bible-study class, where she was helped spiritually and found some very good friends. Other women become hospital volunteers, work with abused children, go back to school, start businesses, or work part-time for someone else. In whatever way she does it, however, any woman who goes through a divorce and comes out whole must somewhere in the process learn to cut the tapes and refocus. Cut the tapes and in essence go on.

The concepts of cut and refocus are really very biblical. Philippians 3:13, 14 (TLB) reads: ". . . Forgetting the past [cutting the tapes] and looking forward to [focusing on] what lies ahead, I strain to reach the end of the race and receive the prize for which God is calling us up to heaven because of what Christ Jesus did for us." "Forgetting" and "looking forward," cutting the old tapes and refocusing: Therein lies half the battle in having peace of mind in the middle of a divorce.

In the middle of all the changes and emotional turmoil of a divorce, perhaps the deepest hurt for the Christian woman is the feeling that she is spiritually alone. Her friends are committed to marriage, and some in her church look down on her for being divorced or even blame her because of some ancient prejudice that assumes when a marriage breaks up it is the woman's fault. The stigma remains, tends to extend to the guiltless as well as the guilty, and presumes to know which is which, even when the evidence is shaky. In some groups a woman's participation in church activities is even restricted; for instance taking part in the communion service may be denied her, even though the Bible clearly teaches that the communion table is the Lord's table and that the prerequisite for any Christian's participation is for him or her to examine himself—and then so eat!

Amy Carmichael hits at the core of God's requirement of Christian love when she says:

God forgive us for the strange coldness of so much of our love. The calculating love of Christians is the shame of the church and the astonishment of angels. By Thine agony and bloody sweat; by Thy cross and passion; by Thy precious death and burial; by the glorious resurrection and ascension; and by the coming of the Holy Ghost, from the sin of coldness, Good Lord, deliver us.

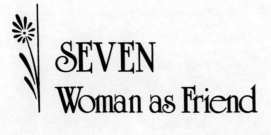

SEVEN
Woman as Friend

My childhood family was one of those old-fashioned ones where aunts and uncles frequently came to our house for Sunday dinner. The visits that my parents, sister, and I made in return to their houses were a source of endless delight to me as a child. Memories of picking Swiss chard from my aunt Esther's garden, when I was very small, and watching "Gunsmoke" and "I Love Lucy" on the television screen at the same aunt's house after my uncle Blanton and I had first served everyone a huge oatmeal bowl full of ice cream, in a day when neither television nor ice cream were everyday commodities: These are the kind of simple things that made up the everyday fabric of our very closely knit, midwestern family.

My mother, in particular, had always taught me the value of family, the importance of relatives. "Your family will be there for you when you really need them," she would say in essence, "even when friends may not come through." With fifteen gathered around the table at Thanksgiving each year, her assumption seemed reasonable. Yet even as a small child something guarded me from a total belief in what she had said about the family; for way down inside me, I knew that nothing on this earth was that sure, except for God Himself. I knew that someday they would all be gone and that I, particularly as the youngest, could be left alone. I didn't dwell on these possibilities. Indeed, I barely acknowledged them. But my awareness was one way in which God prepared me for a time ahead when my worst fears of loss would come true.

During my mother's illness and death, following a car accident, I learned anew of the value of friendship. This family, which had seemed forever, was gone. For in the decade preceding the accident many had died. The accident just completed the losses. Only my aunt Lydia was left, as God's gracious gift to be given for about five years longer, partly, I believe, to ease me through the enormous losses that I had sustained. Yet in her fading memory and increasing physical deterioration it was easy to see that the gift of her life was a very temporary one indeed.

During this time another statement of my mother's came back to me. In those few years before the accident, when so many family members were dying, I had commented from time to time about how scary it was to have almost no family left. She would always reply in the same way: "Don't worry, God will send you other comforters." He did, in part, by showing me anew the remarkable power and faithfulness of friendship. My closer friends became a family now; and while those family members who were present with the Lord were painfully missed, that terrifying sense of desolation, which I had dreaded, never came. The biblical promise that God is no man's debtor had truly been fulfilled, partly through the gift of friendship.

God meets our needs in many ways and through many vehicles: through family, career, friendship, and ultimately through Himself. These are all safety zones from which our lives draw support. To me a safety zone is a person, place, thing, or concept that provides an anchor in the vicissitudes of life. It is something into which we retreat from the storm in order to refurbish and go on. It provides stability. It is an anchor.[1] In many of our lives friendship is a very important safety zone.

In January of 1944 World War II was winding down. The annihilation of 6 million Jews as well as millions of others who opposed Hitler's demonic goals had been essentially accomplished. Only one major group of Jews remained in Europe: those in Hungary. In a last, desperate attempt to destroy these Jews, Nazi henchman Adolf Eichmann was sent to Budapest to implement the so-called final solution, the extermination of the Jewish race. A young Swedish diplomat from a rich banking family in Sweden, Raoul Wallenberg, also went to Budapest, but his mission was the opposite of that of Eichmann: Raoul Wallenberg came to save these Jews whom Eichmann wanted to destroy. Putting himself in constant jeopardy, Wallenberg became the angel of hope in a pit of hell. With his Swedish passports, Wallenberg literally pulled Jews off the trains that were to take the Jews to the killing centers. With his personality, which was commanding and unafraid in its approach, and with his use of handsomely decorated Swedish passports and multiple bureaucratic lists, Wallenberg was able to outwit the Nazis. He knew that the Germans admired power and respected artistic skill.

Wallenberg's native Sweden had remained neutral in its official political posture, but the Swedish people themselves had for some time openly opposed the Nazis. Ultimately,

Wallenberg himself rescued anywhere from 30,000 to 100,000 Jews in Hungary, depending on whose figures you accept.

Personally, however, his actions ultimately cost Raoul Wallenberg everything. For after surviving repeated attempts on his life by the Nazis, and Eichmann in particular, for well over forty years now Raoul Wallenberg has languished and perhaps died in a Soviet prison, after he was taken prisoner by the same Soviet troops who "liberated" Budapest. Wallenberg had understood the Nazi mind and had always outwitted the Gestapo; but unfortunately he had underestimated the treachery of the Soviet army, who were, after all, trusted as part of the Allied forces.

According to Wallenberg biographer Kati Marton, in her book *Wallenberg,* just before the Soviet "liberation" of Hungary at the end of World War II, Raoul Wallenberg was beginning to feel the effects of his 100 percent commitment to rescuing this last group of Jews in Europe. Says Marton: "Wallenberg was exhausted, physically from lack of sleep, emotionally from the strain of having to maintain constant composure amid a daily nightmare. There were so many people leaning on him. . . ."[2] Often, too, it was difficult to find those with whom he could share the tremendous burdens he carried. Yet if a man ever lived who needed the safety zone of friendship, it was Raoul Wallenberg in those months in Budapest.

There were several exceptions to this lack of understanding friends. Among them, his chauffeur, Vilmos Langfelder, was Jewish; and like others at that time, Langfelder had been taken away from his job as an engineer and made to do forced labor. Wallenberg secured Langfelder's freedom, and in turn, he drove for Wallenberg. Langfelder had a calm manner and was temperamentally well suited to work with this reserved Swede. His knowledge of Hungarian also proved to be invaluable. At the end, when Wallenberg was a marked man, both in the eyes of the Nazis and the Russians, Langfelder remained loyal and stayed with him. Langfelder provided a safety zone of support, actual and emotional.

Another anchor of friendship was Wallenberg's Swedish companion, Per Anger. Anger went with him on many rescue missions and shared his commitment. But Anger's intensity was considerably less than that of Wallenberg. He, like Langfelder, exerted a calming effect on Wallenberg. His relationship, too, was a safety zone.

Perhaps more than anyone else, however, Anger could see through the Swedish facade of stoicism and knew that Raoul Wallenberg could not walk on water, anymore than anyone else. Anger knew Wallenberg needed the safety zone of space and relaxation.

Anger knew about Wallenberg's love of nature and his passion for endless hikes in the woods. He also knew the Swede had not had a break from his grueling routine since he arrived five months before. Anger persuaded Wallenberg to join him for a weekend at his retreat at the top of the Svab Hill. "It will be so pleasant," Wallenberg told his secretary, "just to explore the forest for hours on end . . . not to hear the city." For once he did not want to tell her where he could be reached, so badly did he need the rest. But as he was leaving he called back from the door, "Take down this number, Mrs. Falk, just in case. . . ." He had not yet unpacked his bag at the Angers' when the first emergency call reached him. It was the week before Christmas and Wallenberg would not have another chance to explore the woods of Budapest or any other woods again.[3]

To me it is illustrative of the brutal turns of fate that so often marked this man's life, and the incident shows so graphically our human need for safety zones if we are truly to go on with effectiveness.

In spite of the fact that he was unable to make full use of them, support of certain friends who were uniquely tuned in to what Wallenberg was doing in Hungary provided a safety zone that must have given him some degree of comfort even as he was slipped away into the darkness of the Soviet prison system. At least their understanding gave him recent, positive memories for years to come. And his relationship with these people is certainly an eloquent statement of both the need for and the meaning of safety zones, particularly as they involve the safety zones of friendship.

Yet sometimes we lose our safety zones. That was the case in my own life at the time my mother died. If at such a time we are conscious of the fact that the loss, or the potential loss, involves the diminishing of our supply of safety zones, we can then go on to cultivate old safety zones or find new ones, so that the feeling of loss is not so great. Raoul Wallenberg did not have the immediate security and comfort of his Swedish family, once he came to Budapest, although the memories of them undoubtedly remained as a very important safety zone throughout his life. So rather than pulling back into a sort of isolated self-pity, Wallenberg used the safety zone of valued friends with whom he shared an important work for humanity. He also contributed to his safety zone of positive memories.

In contrast, an acquaintance of mine lost her husband to cancer and was urged by a psychotherapist to leave her job and sell her house within months after the death. The result was a deep depression, bordering on suicide. The cause of the depression was the loss of major safety zones, not only in the death of her husband, but in the almost immediate loss of her career and her home, which held many pleasant memories for her. Rather than working toward gaining safety zones after the death of her husband, she was actually counseled to lose them!

Christopher Columbus never left port without several anchors. We, too, should never be without several important safety zones in our lives and many small ones as well, like favorite restaurants, special traditions, absorbing books, pets, special pieces of music, and interesting hobbies into which we can pour our creativeness. For none of us can afford to lose too many safety zones at one time. If we make it a practice to have several major safety zones and many small ones at all times, then if we lose some, we will at least have several others to fall back on, and we will, of course, have the ability to develop new safety zones. Friendship provides a safety zone for most women, and it is therefore important for woman to nurture her relationships with others and keep them in good balance.

We live in a time that is different from that of human beings in any other time. TV commercials advertise dinner in Paris for those who live in places like Los Angeles or New York; and the last time I heard, the average stay for an apartment dweller was six months. House owners remain in one house for an average period under five years. The result is a sort of disposable life-style that does not put down roots. Even those who try to establish long-term residency seem to get caught up in this disposable frame of mind. Recently I heard of a couple approaching retirement who not only sold their house but also sold all their furniture, linen, dishes, and cutlery and bought everything new. All I could think of was how many safety zones they sold! To add new upholstery to the old or to mix new pieces with cherished old pieces: That is to keep valued safety zones while adding new ones. But to just throw away the past, with all its memories, is to dispose of valued safety zones.

If our things and life-styles have become disposable, so have our relationships with people. Marriages are thrown away because we no longer "feel love" or because we have "outgrown" our spouses. Babies are aborted because it's not a convenient time to have them or, as one person expressed to me, because we don't want to be pregnant and fat during a vacation in the Bahamas. And friendships become superficial and not valued properly because, after all, we always anticipate the next move. As one person put it, "Why develop a good friendship only to move and suffer the pain of loss?"

The complexities of the human need for roots, for friends, for permanency in an age of constant change confront the average woman. We can't make the world slow down, but we can learn to deal with this changing world.

One way we can do this is by daring to commit to friendships, in spite of potential geographical moves. For at times the moves do not occur as quickly as they are anticipated anyway, and during that time a good friendship can be a much needed source of encouragement and just plain fun. Also, because of our easy mobility and fast communication, moving does not need to end a friendship. Having a stack of greeting cards on hand for all occasions, and keeping up with distant friends at impulse, without having to go to the store to get the card before you can do it, is one way of nurturing a long-distance friendship. Card shopping in bulk is fun for most women, and when the card is needed, the impulse to send that card will not be destroyed because we don't have time to go to the store.

Telephone calls and brief visits also help in keeping up with a long-range friendship, when money and time make these methods possible. Praying for friends who live far away is another way to help them, be part of their lives, and feel close to them. When the prayer is mutual and each person prays for the other with specific requests and specific praise for answered prayers, the results are felt by both. Such a friendship will not die, even in this age of fast-paced living, but rather it will extend into eternity.

In the same way that some friendships are long-distance, while others involve the person next door, each friendship is unique in what it has to give and in what it demands. It becomes its own special safety zone and requires its own commitment. My mother used to have what she called her telephone friend. The woman had known my mother from years back and was then bedridden. They rarely saw each other in person, but they chatted for long periods on the phone, sometimes encouraging each other, but as often as not just talking about small, everyday things like recipes, small family incidents, and even politics. Theirs was a friendship with a limited scope, the telephone. If some eager, helpful person had tried to make it into something broader and more inclusive, they might have destroyed the friendship; for it flourished as a telephone friendship.

Sometimes it is important to know when to leave things alone. My mother's friendship with her "telephone friend" was, I suspect, a good friendship *because* of its boundaries. Actually in the early years, back in Chicago, when they had been young girls, the friendship had not been that valuable to either. But now, later on in life, as a telephone friendship, it was greatly valued by both. Other friends might be good to shop with or do all the other things friends do, but this friendship had one important uniqueness: It was a telephone friendship.

All of us have friendships that, while they may be broader in scope than just the telephone, meet certain specific needs. Some friends listen well or offer wise advice; others aren't very wise but are fun to be with, sort of adventurous. Then there are those with whom we share a particular issue, such as having children or a specific problem child, or a cause, such as a political candidate or the support of a missionary project. We have friends whom we cherish because we have known them for so many years that they share a past with us. If we met them today, without that common past, we might not even care to be friends, because the specific need that makes the friendship valuable would be gone. In the same way, teachers who might not like each other on Saturday morning, for example, often enjoy each other at noonday lunch, because *then* they have some commonality of interests to share. Surely no one friendship can meet all needs. It is a wise person indeed who can perceive when a friendship can be expanded and when its very boundaries are its strengths. Above all, he or she will realize that while no friendship can be strong in all areas, the factors that any given friendship may lack do not necessarily preclude its value in other areas.

In the area of female-female relationships, as well as in female-male relationships, certain unique problems arise. Paramount in friendships between women is the issue of priorities. When a woman is in love, engaged to be married, or even married, it is important to put the relationship with the man first, while at the same time the relationships which may exist with women should not be discarded. Too many women treat female friends as though they are no longer important, once they have met a man. Then they wonder why when they lose that man, or even when he is away for a short trip, no one else is there for them.

Well-known mystery writer P. D. James gives us a telling description of the loneliness of a career woman, an assistant English detective, who more or less dumped all her female friends for a man and her career, then suddenly needed them:

By evening she had been seized by a desperate need for human companionship. . . . Before she became Paul's mistress she had spent a fair proportion of her spare time with Emma, quick lunches at a pub or cafe convenient for both their offices, films, the occasional theatre, even a weekend together in Amsterdam to visit the Rijksmuseum. It had been an undemanding, unconfiding friendship. She had known that Emma would never give up the chance of a date with a man to spend an evening with her; and Emma had been the first victim to her obsessional need for privacy, the reluctance to commit even an hour of time which could be given to Paul. She looked at her watch. It was six forty-two. Unless Emma was spending the weekend out of town she would probably be at home.

She had to look up the number. The familiar digits sprang from the page at her like a key to an earlier, half-forgotten existence. She hadn't spoken to a human being since the police had left, and she wondered if her voice sounded as gruff and false to Emma as it did to her own ears.

"Hello? Emma? You won't believe it. This is Carole, Carole Washburn."

There was the sound of music, joyous, contrapuntal. It could have been Bach or Vivaldi. Emma called: "Turn it down, darling," and then to Carole: "Good God! How are you?"

"Fine. It's been ages since we met. I wondered if you'd like to see a film or something. Tonight perhaps."

There was a small silence, and then Emma's voice, carefully uncommitted, surprise and perhaps a small note of resentment carefully controlled.

"Sorry, we've got people coming in for dinner."

Emma had always said dinner rather than supper even when they were proposing to eat a take-away Chinese meal at the kitchen table. It had been one of those minor snobberies which Carole had found irritating. She said: "Next weekend perhaps?"

"Not possible, I'm afraid. Alistair and I are driving down to Wiltshire. Visiting his parents, actually. Another time perhaps. Lovely to hear from you. I must fly, the guests are due at seven-thirty. I'll give you a ring sometime."

It was all she could do not to cry out: "Include me, include me! Please, I need to come." The receiver was replaced, voice, music, communication cut off. . . . And Emma wouldn't ring back. She had Alistair; a shared life, shared friends. You couldn't cut people out of your life and expect to find them complaisant, readily available, just because you needed to feel human again.[4]

If unique problems exist in friendships between women, the possibility for problems becomes even greater in relationships, apart from marriage, that exist between women and men. Yet it is certainly healthy and even biblical for such relationships to exist, and many of us have known nonromantic relationships with the opposite sex that have been morally correct and emotionally satisfying.

One evening a few years ago my friend Jim and I became deeply engrossed as we explored the possibilities for helping teenagers on drugs. Jim's wife, Edith, had been as involved as we, until the phone rang and she was trapped for a good forty-five minutes.

Now as she filled our coffee cups for the fifth time and rejoined us, she, too, became involved again. Ideas seemed to flow as the hours went by: ideas on rehabilitation; thoughts for a new book (actually this incident occurred right before I wrote my first book, *Where Do I Go to Buy Happiness?*); even an exciting idea for making educational cassettes (an idea that did not materialize!). Above all, the three of us were close and united in our thoughts and feelings. We had a good friendship, male and female, between us. Suddenly I looked up at the clock: 2:00 A.M.! Since I had to get up early the next morning, I hurriedly got up to leave. We had been brainstorming for six hours—and to each of us it had seemed like just two hours.

On the way home I thought about the great relationship the three of us had, and the friendship was just as close with Edith as it was with Jim.

A friend once said to me: "I don't believe a woman can have a friendship with a man other than her husband. It always becomes too involved." Yet it is hard for me to feel that a woman's role in friendship should be restricted to her husband, if she has one, and to her female friends.

To the contrary, while there are potential problems inherent in relationships between women and men, when they are not married to each other, such relationships can also be healthy and vital. Furthermore, no women, married or single, can entirely avoid these relationships. They will occur if a woman is in the business world in almost any capacity. They are present in the activities that couples engage in, unless those activities are strictly limited to couples only. Even then there will be the intermingling of men and women with other men and women who are not their marriage partners. Furthermore, for all concerned, whether married, single, widowed, or divorced, friendships with members of the opposite sex are important in a well-rounded social life. Few women enjoy only the exclusive company of women.

Years ago, when I was teaching tenth graders in high school, I often overheard teenagers giggle when the word *love* was mentioned, because they always associated love with sex, usually forbidden sex. Yet embarrassment and confusion regarding the word *love* are not just teenage peculiarities. They carry over into adulthood. I recently watched several adults playing a game in which, if you arrive at a certain space, you are required to tell someone you love him or her, if you have not already used that word during the day. A bit silly? Perhaps. But certainly not life threatening—and that is exactly the way most people responded. Some refused to say it; one clenched his hands, looked upward at the ceiling, and choked out the words!

At its most basic level, love is a feeling of closeness toward someone, a sense of warmth, a desire to enjoy that person's company. Certainly this at times includes sexual attraction toward someone of the opposite sex, but that fact does not preclude a relationship with the opposite sex that does not include romantic attachment. *Love* is not synonymous with *sex*. Loving is not synonymous with being *in love*. At times it is not easy to keep out the romantic element, but it is possible; and it is important in the area of friendship for women to guard against crossing, even mentally, that line between healthy, God-given friendship and a romantic involvement.

Grasping the concept that while it is not always easy to keep the romantic element out of a male-female relationship, it is possible, will free some women to increase the breadth of some of their relationships. Other women will perhaps be challenged to stop ruining good relationships with the excuse that they "just can't help it" when their feelings get out of control! They *can* help it! For it is possible for men and women to have meaningful relationships apart from sexual involvement. Thus a married woman may find a friend in a married man, or a single woman may value a relationship with a married man, without adversely affecting anyone's marriage.

One woman I know has no male friends except her husband. Oh, she knows a few men, but there are no real relationships involved. She has bluntly verbalized a deep fear of being close to a man, because "friendships with men don't work."

In contrast, in a school where I once taught, there were several married men, another unmarried woman, and myself who became good friends. We had parties on people's birthdays and used to get into philosophical debates during lunch. There were honest discussions involving school problems, how we each felt about our goals in life, and even personal needs. Sometimes someone would have a particular problem, like the day that one member of the group had to put an elderly relative into a convalescent home, and we all tried to give that person some support.

At the time I was deeply involved in working with a large number of students on drugs, which was a very demanding job. I can't count the times that one of those men would come and drag me away for lunch, because he knew I needed the break, or the times one of them would "cover" for me in a class so that I could finish talking to a student who needed me. That, too, was love; but not romantic love, for none of us was *in* love with any of the others. In fact, some of the happiest times we had were at Christmas, when we would get together for dinner and include dates and wives. We were all just close friends, and to a degree we will always be so.

For me as a single woman, the closeness of a group that included both men and women was important. Previously I had taught in a girls' school, where the company of only females lacked something. As an unmarried woman my needs include male relationships. Sometimes that means I get hurt, because I start to feel something deeper than friendship toward someone who can't return that feeling. But I have found that such feelings can be controlled a great deal more completely than most of us care to admit. They can always be walked away from rather than indulged. At times, too, someone feels deeply toward me and I am unable to return the feelings and allow the relationship to deepen, either because he is already married or because for a variety of reasons I do not feel that we are suited for each other. Thus risk and hurt are part of life if one is truly alive; yet without them one lives an isolated, safe existence where the risk is minimal, but so are the joy and fulfillment.

Married women, too, profit from male relationships. One woman I know has an interesting, attentive husband. They share their feelings and have many common interests. Yet a certain philanthropic project of hers evokes little interest from him. Another friend and his wife spend a good deal of time talking with her and giving her suggestions in this area, and in this way she gets a male as well as a female viewpoint. Both couples are good friends, and there is no jealousy.

Women in this culture are still somewhat conditioned to feel that there is strength in male support during a crisis and that a male viewpoint on business affairs is often more objective and knowledgeable. For whatever the reason, these feelings seem to prevail. Years ago, immediately following the death of my newborn baby nephew, which hit me harder than anyone in my family ever realized, a male friend took me from the hospital to the beach for dinner. He knew the beach was my safety zone, and at that time I wanted the support of his male strength. I wanted him, not a girl friend.

During my father's terminal illness, following two massive strokes, I needed different kinds of support: the luncheon chats with a close girl friend and the valuable before-I-went-to-bed telephone calls from another close female friend. Yet when my father was alive, it was his advice I wanted on financial matters, not my mother's. Since his death, I have always had several male friends to whom I can turn when I need business advice. I have women who fill this need, too, but even when my female friends give almost the same advice, I tend to believe the men more. I'm not saying that such an attitude is logical, but I believe it is the way many women still feel. While it is important not to minimize the business potential many women possess, it is of equal importance to admit, perhaps contradictorily, that sometimes some women just need the strengthening reassurance of a man on these subjects, in the same way that men often find themselves in need of female comfort in other areas.

Many of the more superficial differences between men and women at this time are probably still cultural. But unless they actually detract from the real rights of women, they should not be construed as a denigration of women. While I personally am in full support of women's rights in job opportunity, for example, I would not enjoy living in a culture where I was treated the same as a man. I like to have a man open a door for me, not only if he's in love with me, but also if he just respects me as a woman. Conversely, I'm not adverse to serving him coffee, as long as it's appreciated, not demanded. What I don't enjoy is being walked over in rent raises or book contracts or having my opinion ignored in issues of substance because I'm a woman. Women are different from men, and both men and women should enjoy these differences, but this does not mean that women have less general value than men. Upon this premise lies a good relationship between a man and woman.

From a biblical point of view, repeatedly in the New Testament Paul refers to the women who worked with him. They were not merely business colleagues, for often he stayed in their homes when he traveled or when he was ill, and these women nursed him in his illness. Yet Paul was single, at least during part of this time, and many of these women were married. Therefore, there seems to be the attitude, from the life of Paul as well as from other biblical examples, that men and women can be close friends without romantic involvement.

For the woman who chooses to have good friendships with men, apart from marriage, there are certain moral obligations. It is important to appear right before the world around you, even when you yourself know that there is no wrongdoing. This fits into Paul's admonitions not to cause your brother to stumble and to avoid all appearance of evil. It is vital that in relating to a married man a woman scrupulously avoids behavior that could hurt the man's spouse and especially their marriage. Good counsel in this respect could be that it is wise, when possible, to have a closer relationship with the wife than with her husband. When this is impossible, the wise female friend will consider the wife's feelings above her own friendship with the wife's husband, for their marriage is always more important than the single friendship of either spouse.

For example, a while back, before they moved away, I had a friendship with a couple who are about the same age as I am. One weekend Jeannette took their three children and went to visit her mother. Joe, her husband, was left home alone. Lonely, he called me and asked me to go to a concert. Jeannette knew and approved, he said. After all, I myself knew that Joe and I were only friends. Yet I knew that in recent days Jeannette and Joe had been quarreling quite alot. Also, Joe and I had been together quite a few times working on a project in the school in which we both taught, and more than once Joe had made disparaging remarks about Jeannette. It was better, I decided, for Joe to have dinner with his brother or someone else, not me. I didn't want to ruin a good relationship, nor did I want to in any way contribute to the unhappiness that already existed in their marriage.

Sex, too, may become an issue if a woman and man become friends—even if they are both married. Even if the man and woman are both single, a sexual relationship is not acceptable by scriptural standards. Biblically the sexual act epitomizes the highest expression of love within a marriage and is paralleled with the union of Christ and His church. It is, therefore, not an act that should be lightly engaged in because of the physical and emotional desires of the moment. Here the single woman may have a greater problem than the married woman, for the married woman presumably has her sexual needs met by her husband. But for the single woman or the married woman who is having marital difficulties, sexual needs may at times be great.

To be true to her beliefs, she must have an automatic mind-set toward the will of God that biblically there is no possibility of God's approval of sex outside marriage. Unpopular as the phrase may be in some circles, *extramarital sex* is still called sin by God.

Even apart from Christianity, sex outside of marriage is not a satisfactory situation. Women in particular interpret sexual intercourse as a preliminary to a permanent relationship. When it does not prove to be more than a short-range affair, a woman may feel deeply rejected and unlovable. For the Christian woman there are the added problems of guilt and feelings of spiritual alienation from both Christian friends and God. One woman I know who has been sexually involved with a married man has given up all her Christian friends, because she can't face them. Another can't feel free in her devotional life with God, because she knows that she is in direct conflict with His will. Any women whom I have talked to who are having premarital or extramarital affairs and who are evangelical in their beliefs seem to live lives of carefully contrived secrecy, which are not in themselves conducive to good mental health.

Only as a woman has a daily, deeply committed mind-set toward the will of God in this area of friendship will she be most able to have good male-female relationships without the romantic element taking over. It is important, too, for women to guard against the currently popular notion that somehow whatever we feel we must do. Or worse still, whatever feels good must be right, because if we feel good we are doing right.

While the friendships women have with one another and

with men each have certain unique blessings and obligations, friendship itself has a universality in its composition.
For all of us who are Christians, whether we are male or
female, can at times echo the feeling of C. S. Lewis in his
words:

> . . . It will seem to us that . . . we four or five . . . have
> chosen one another, the insight of each finding the intrinsic
> beauty of the rest . . . in reality a few year's difference in the
> dates of our births, a few more miles between certain
> houses, the choice of one university instead of another . . .
> any of these chances might have kept us apart. But, for a
> Christian there are, strictly speaking, no chances. A secret
> Master of Ceremonies has been at work. Christ who said to
> the disciples, "Ye have not chosen me, *but* I have chosen
> you," can truly say to every group of Christian friends, "You
> have not chosen one another, but I have chosen you for one
> another."

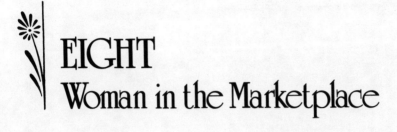

EIGHT
Woman in the Marketplace

$\bigwedge$ small boy made a last frantic effort to win at the new game the two of us were both playing for the first time. To play the game involved both luck and organized thinking. My eight-year-old friend needed the experience of winning, so I hoped that, with a final stroke of luck, he would defeat me. However, I was ahead, and to fake losing would have been such an obvious deception that John's victory would have been a hollow one. So reluctantly, with a last right move, I won the game. Angrily John looked over at me and exclaimed: "Don't you know, girls aren't supposed to beat boys?"

"Girls aren't supposed to beat boys" is unfortunately the viewpoint of many adults, both male and female; and children pick up the idea at a very early age. Nor is this concept an outdated male chauvinistic idea, for many women feel exactly the same way. I hear women say things like: "Don't explain the insurance to me; I don't understand things like that. My husband handles those matters." Or, "I don't understand Bible doctrine. I leave that to my husband. I just try to be a good wife," as though somehow being a "good wife" implies low intelligence as a prerequisite! Yet any one of these same women is offended if someone overtly doubts her intelligence, or she becomes confused if her husband, after ten years of marriage, turns to another woman because "she can talk to me."

The fact is many men want a woman who is their intellectual equal. A man who has a good self-image will not need to have a spouse who is inferior to himself, in order to boost his own deflated ego. He will want to share the responsibilities of marriage, and he will desire a woman with whom he can converse intelligently.

While there are men who feel threatened by bright women, it is their defective egos rather than their spiritual prowess that shapes their fears. In the long run a bright woman who "plays dumb" to get a man will probably not build a very good marriage. Her intelligence will eventually show and offend her husband, or she will play the "dumb role" throughout a miserable and unchallenging marriage.

Many in our society still place a greater value on male intelligence. A girl's education is not always considered as important as a boy's, because after all a girl can always grow up, get married, and be supported by her husband. Being supported in a marriage is a perfectly acceptable role for a woman, *if* that is her choice in life rather than a role she accepts as inevitable because she is a woman.

I am at times in social situations where I can perhaps be momentarily a little detached in my observations of the conversations between married couples. Sometimes I don't know the people very well, which creates a shyness of sorts in me and therefore detaches me for the moment. Very often in such situations I notice the frequency with which the male viewpoint predominates just because it is the male viewpoint.

As an example, recently I had dinner with a couple. The man began to voice his strong anti-Semitic views. Outraged, I argued back. In contrast, his wife just sat there, not agreeing with him, but afraid to argue against him. She allowed his opinion to prevail with her while she offered a feeble statement of objection: "Well, dear, are you sure you really feel that way?" He was sure! So the topic was dropped.

Furthermore, it seems, that while women are equal in intelligence to men, that intellectual ability is not always as carefully nurtured in them as it is in their male counterparts. Marriage or the prospect of marriage should not stop a woman's development, nor should men automatically be given jobs involving high-powered thinking. A girl of sixteen who against her inclination plans a secretarial future, because that's what is expected of her, should reconsider. If she prefers to become a lawyer and has that kind of ability, why should she become anything else? On the other hand, if a young boy is expected to be educated toward joining his father's law firm but prefers interior decorating and has real talent for that, why shouldn't he do what he is best suited for? Why should women be file clerks and waitresses, while men study for law, medicine, or engineering? To go further, what's wrong with a lady plumber, if that's what she wants to be? She'll make a lot more money working with pipes than from most so-called women's jobs. Don't argue that being a plumber is not ladylike or is too degrading! Not unless you remove all the underpaid women who clean toilets in public institutions or those that clean up in convalescent homes and hospitals!

Yet as firmly as I believe in women and men both being free to do a job for which they have interest and

talent, I do not feel good about these jobs being given or
taken as mere tokens. For being a token person in a
place of employment implies that something other than
your ability got you the job. You never have the chance
to know if you could have obtained the position on your
own. It is, therefore, as denigrating to be accepted for a
job just because you're a woman as it is to be rejected for
the same reason.

A while back, when it became obvious that women could
handle anchoring a television news show as well as men,
and when the pressure on the networks had accelerated to
the point where women could apparently no longer be
ignored, within a short period of time one woman appeared
on each major evening news presentation. Never three
women and no men, or two women and one man, or just
three good men. It is hard for me to believe that out of all
the people interested in that kind of a job, one woman was
always better than the competing male applicants or that at
times a second woman might not have been better than the
male newscaster who got the job.

The same token approach has been true in the history of
the civil-rights movement. Blacks at first appeared, one by
one. One in a food commercial, one in a documentary, one
in a given law firm or a school faculty. Races that didn't
complain, like the Orientals or the American Indians, were
rarely seen at all. They didn't require a token to silence them,
so they didn't even get the token, much less full equality.

Tokens in the marketplace are a necessary start, I suppose. Indeed many jobs which were originally given as
token offerings to women are now offered equally to men
and women alike. Yet I still don't like the idea of tokens. It
would be nice to think sex and race didn't matter in getting
a job in this enlightened time of ours. In a country such as

ours, where competition has always been so important, it would be admirable if people went into a vocation and got jobs because they were good at what they do and well trained, not because they were women or not women.

Many Christians view the home, the kitchen, and the church as the only places where the Christian woman may function if she is to be in the will of God. Yet such a viewpoint is not, in my opinion, consistent with sound biblical exegesis. Women, like men, have certain unique roles that are delineated in a broad sense throughout the Scriptures and that are, at times, even dictated by nature. Within that scope, each man and woman born into this world has a uniqueness of function that he or she alone can discern from God.

Three women, one in the Old Testament and two in the New Testament, provide a sampling of biblical examples on the subject. These were godly women in every sense of the word. But they show graphically the broad spectrum of choice God has given to woman with regard to her specific role at any given time in her life.

Deborah became a leader in Israel when King Jabin of Canaan was making life unbearable for Israel. In Judges 4:3 (TLB) we read that he had "made life unbearable for the Israelis for twenty years."

Deborah was the wife of Lappidoth. Apparently during that time she was also a person to whom many people came for counsel. At the peak of the problem with Jabin, Deborah called a top military leader, Barak, and told him of the need to defeat Jabin's army and his general, Sisera.

After they drew up plans, Barak agreed to go after Jabin, but with one stipulation: "I'll go, but only if you go with me" (v. 8 TLB).

Deborah agreed, but with a counter warning: ". . . I'll go

with you; but I'm warning you now that the honor of conquering Sisera will go to a woman instead of to you! . . ." (v.
9 TLB).

Their efforts were successful. Deborah's military orders
proved effective and ". . . after that there was peace in the
land for forty years" (5:31 TLB).

While Deborah was a politician and military leader, another woman, Lydia, who lived after the time of Christ, was
a businesswoman. Acts 16:14 (TLB) describes her as a
". . . saleswoman from Thyatira, a merchant of purple
cloth. . . ." Whether or not she was married is not stated in
the Bible, but it seems clear that her business was both
successful and her own. She was a Christian businesswoman.

After her conversion to Christianity, Lydia's acceptance
by such church leaders as Paul and Silas is made obvious by
the fact that they came and stayed at her home. Her home
probably became something of a haven for them, since they
returned there again later, after their release from jail.

Priscilla was different from both Deborah and Lydia. This
Jewish woman left Rome with her husband, Aquila, as a
result of Jewish persecution. They finally ended up in
Ephesus, where both of them earned a living as tentmakers.

Both Priscilla and her husband were very involved in the
New Testament church, and apparently they were well
taught in New Testament doctrine. For when Apollos came
to speak at Ephesus, they recognized his lack of New Testament knowledge and "afterwards they met with him and
explained what had happened to Jesus since the time of
John, and all that it meant!" (Acts 18:26 TLB). Yet Apollos
himself was already considered a remarkable Bible teacher.

That Priscilla herself was considered an intelligent and
powerful woman in the early church is further proven by

historical facts other than those recorded in the Bible. According to *All of the Women of the Bible*, by Edith Deen:

> Tertullian records, "By the holy Prisca, the gospel is preached." One of the oldest catacombs of Rome—the Coemeterium Priscilla, was named in her honor. And a church, "Titulus St. Prisca," was erected on the Aventine in Rome. It bore the inscription "Titulus Aquila et Prisca." Prisca's name appears often on monuments of Rome. And "Acts of St. Prisc" was a legendary writing popular in the tenth century.

A politician and military leader, Deborah; a successful businesswoman who owned her own home, Lydia; and a church leader, Priscilla: All three gave every evidence of superior intellect. All three had great qualities of leadership. At least two of the three functioned in the marketplace. Yet all three kept their own homes, were better than average as hostesses in those homes, and at least two were married. Their lives seemed to reinforce the idea that women are capable of performing superior intellectual tasks, and furthermore, from a scriptural point of view, such performance is appropriate. One gets the feeling that any of these three women, if they were taken out of the safety of the ancient biblical history and placed in various evangelical churches today, might well intimidate certain contemporary masculine members of the clergy who believe that woman should indeed not be in the marketplace.

Pastors and other church personnel who do not believe that the Bible warrants women working should probably not be counseling single parents who must work, nor in my opinion should they be so quick to judge even women who do have a choice, since there are so many notable exceptions to their beliefs in the Scriptures. It is one thing to agree to disagree; it is quite another to use the authority of the pastorate to inflict guilt and perhaps influence women to turn away from a God-given calling. It is an awesome thing to tamper with God's will for an individual's life!

We may safely assume God does not ordinarily waste talent that He has given. Both men and women have varying degrees of intellectual ability and other talents, such as ability in art. If a woman finds that she has both the ability and the inclination to contribute something to society, she should not be held back because she is a woman. Nor should a man be pushed ahead into an area for which he is not suited, just because he is a man.

In a church I once attended a young man was urged to become Sunday-school superintendent because "he was such a good Christian." He *was* a good Christian, but he completely lacked creativity and was not particularly sensitive to the needs of children. To make sure that he didn't completely fail, his wife carefully planned each Sunday's program with him, and he faithfully followed her instructions. When a special program was approaching, she would always plan the format for him. He never learned how to do it on his own, but I was always amused when I heard someone compliment him for an idea that was never his in the first place.

The truly sad part lay in the effect it had on the marriage. Instead of doing something he could do well, the husband felt inadequate functioning as a puppet. Yet he knew that to play such a role was his only way of survival in the job he had taken on. He never got a chance to use the talents God had uniquely given him. His wife, on the other hand, felt a little angry at having to hide her ability and frustrated because she knew the effect the whole situation was having on her husband. For as much as he needed her, he also resented her and felt denigrated by the whole situation.

It is unrealistic to assume that men are always brighter than women. Knowing that fact and yet playing the role of the intellectually deficient wife or the all-knowing male is plain stupid. In contrast to such false role play, when a man and a woman who have a good relationship interact in a more relaxed way, both will exhibit their strong and weak points to varying degrees, yet neither will feel threatened by the other. To role play only makes a relationship shallow and unnatural, or at times it only prolongs an unrewarding friendship between people who probably are so incompatible that they wouldn't be friends if they really let down with each other.

There are, however, unique problems confronted by a woman who enters the marketplace, particularly if she is married and even more so if she has young children. A woman who has a job she goes to a certain number of hours each week or a woman who writes at home or does crafts or runs for a political office will often find these duties running in conflict with her role as wife and mother. There is little difference here between a woman performing her duties as wife and mother and that of the businessman who has no time for his family because he gets overinvolved in his work, except that biblically the female task of mothering does seem to involve more time from her, which is spent with the children in nurturing, than it does from the father. Either parent, however, must balance any outside work with family responsibilities. Neither can just add on jobs and responsibilities, leaving little time and energy to do any one of them well, without some scars resulting in their marriage and with their children.

Thus whether it comes by better organization, extra help

from a maid or gardener, or by just learning to say no to even "good" demands, any woman needs to be careful that in developing some of her abilities she doesn't just add to an already overburdened schedule. One woman I know maintains a large house and garden, takes her son to frequent baseball practices and games and Boy Scout activities, takes her daughter to Brownies and piano lessons, and makes frequent trips to the orthodontist. Add to these, grocery shopping, cooking, trips for shoe repair and to the cleaner's, countless impromptu errands here and there, and you have a schedule that is already too full. Car pools for the children and a declaration that trips to places like the cleaner's and the grocery store will only be made at a certain time each week will help preserve precious time and energy that can better be used elsewhere.

Assuming that she has a choice, both for the nurturing of the children and for her own sanity and enjoyment, a woman who has children should probably deeply consider any decision to work for any length of time each week out of the home when her children are still young. The woman who does work full-time, however, will then need the complete cooperation of her husband, children, and perhaps family in general. Often a woman is expected to work by a husband who wants her to earn extra money, but then she is still expected to fulfill all the normal tasks of the home that she did before she assumed an outside job.

One woman I know is urged to work full-time by her husband, yet he balks at any suggestion that he help with the housework. He still expects things to be brought to him on demand, along with gourmet dinners served upon his arrival home. In all fairness, both sides can be unreasonable when it comes to dividing up the tasks. One man often cleans or cooks on his time off, only to be told that he's not doing it right. Justifiably this man's response to his wife is that if she controls the housework, then she can do it. If they share the housework, they also share in saying how it will be done. So far this particular woman has chosen to do it all rather than to relinquish her say in how it's done. As a result her over-work has become her problem rather than that of her husband, who is willing to help her, but not to be dictated to.

In contrast some couples work out the division of labor very equitably. A woman who spends a great deal of time in artistic endeavors does them late at night when the children are in bed. In order to let her sleep later in the morning, her husband regularly gets up and makes breakfast. Since she is home in the afternoon and uses that time to be with her children, she makes sure that each evening she has an inviting dinner for her husband at the time of day when he is most tired and appreciates the attention. In this way they support each other's endeavors and show mutual love. The wife is not deprived of her own pursuits, and as a result she is a happier person and a better marriage partner.

Each person has a unique life, a unique set of priorities and tasks. Any two people who join together in marriage thus have a unique relationship. There is no stamped-out life-style that will work for every individual or for every marriage. Each person, each marriage, and each job is unique in its demands and rewards.

Apart from the adjustments of family and work load, woman in the marketplace does face some problems unique from those men encounter, because she is indeed different from man. She is *woman!* When a woman pretends there is no difference between her and men, she makes a major mistake, for by accepting her uniqueness as a woman and dealing with the resultant problems, she will deal most effectively in the marketplace.

For example, one way in which some women have made it to the top, so to speak, has been by their willingness to sleep with certain pivotal men. I am not saying that this pattern has not been reversed to a situation where a female executive has required this from a man if he wished to be promoted. Yet traditionally the man has required it of the woman. Many women have responded by giving in to the male demands, which is obviously not an answer any Christian woman can conscientiously accept. Others have resisted to the point of trying to be unattractive or even masculinized in their approach, so that everyone becomes the same, male and female. Yet everyone will never be the same. Nor should any woman wish to lose her gracefulness and appeal as a woman in order to be promoted without sexual harassment. For it is possible to be gracious yet firm in one's refusal of sexual advances.

Once when I was at a convention, I engaged in a conversation with a man who had not seen his wife for several weeks and was obviously homesick for both her and his children. After a relatively short time, the man rather abruptly asked me to go to bed with him. What held me in good stead was that I had already formed a mind-set of saying no to such offers. So in spite of his attractiveness, my only real problem was how to say no. My reply went something like, "Wouldn't you feel better tomorrow when you see your wife and children if we just had another cup of coffee and called it quits?" He seemed almost relieved, and he hadn't been insulted by my refusal. Unfortunately, sometimes a woman has to use greater bluntness than this man demanded of me.

Nor are Christian men necessarily exceptions to the general rule. In all my years in the marketplace, the most obnoxious man I ever had to turn down was a Christian, who temporarily caused me loss in the business world by my refusal and who required out-and-out rudeness from me in order to get rid of him. No business deal is worth the price tag of giving one's body.

If God really wants something for us, He will give it without our having to commit sin. If we have a mind-set for the will of God, sexual harassment will not be so hard to deal with.

While the marketplace presents problems unique to woman, it also confers its honors and fulfillment. Furthermore, every woman should pursue the interests and talents God has given her. Whether it be by a method as undramatic as reading a book each afternoon or evening or as dramatic as an outside job, it will tend to raise her feelings of worth and thus better her relationship with others, including her family.

For women who have to work to support themselves but don't enjoy that work, or for women who feel dissatisfied with household tasks consuming all their lives, the pursuit of something else that interests them will add greater meaning to their lives. I have known women who have added meaning to their lives by working part-time with handicapped children or teaching a Bible study or doing various art projects. Some have written magazine articles, worked for political campaigns, and engaged in any number of other activities that have greatly enhanced their lives.

For some women the answer to their intellectual fulfillment will be in a full-time commitment to a career. Others may successfully combine a career with a marriage, if they keep in mind that they cannot do it all at one time. Still others will find most of their fulfillment within the home, yet they will wisely develop other interests that will keep them from stagnating. Each woman must find fulfillment in her own way. But she should not be limited by the notion that as a woman she is not intellectually suited for competition with men.

For contemporary woman, it is the best of times; it is the worst of times. It is new; it is old. After World War II there was a resurgence of women who worked full-time outside of the home. Yet woman in the marketplace is not new. For woman has been in the marketplace for centuries. It was just new to us in this culture at that time.

Throughout the history of mankind, women have always held positions of power and influence. In certain cultures they have even been the ruling sex. And certainly biblical woman was always considered equal to man in worth and responsible in position. Yet within our own country's history we women have only recently come into our own, so to speak; and while that position has given us status and material independence, if we are not vigilant, it can take away from us something of the respect and honor that the word *woman* has at its best commanded.

For even as I write these words I realize anew that the definition of the character of God's woman has not really changed that much in the two millennia since our Lord walked this earth. Oh, woman's status has changed on the surface, and that change has been of great importance to all of us, whether or not we are conscious of it. There are cultural differences between that time and now, the opportunities in some areas are greater today, and certainly there is a general sense of more complete equality in this century. Yet to be woman is still most fully expressed, even for today, as it was in ancient times in the biblical description included at the end of the book of Proverbs. In answer to the age-old question: "Who can find a virtuous woman? for her price is far above rubies," the passage provides a lengthy list of descriptions of God's woman, including:

The heart of her husband doth safely trust in her. . . .

She considereth a field, and buyeth it: with the fruit of her hands she planteth a vineyard. . . .

She perceiveth that her merchandise is good: her candle goeth not out by night. . . .

She stretcheth out her hand to the poor. . . .

She maketh herself coverings of tapestry. . . .

She maketh fine linen and selleth it. . . .

Strength and honour are her clothing. . . . She openeth her mouth with wisdom; and in her tongue is the law of kindness.

She looketh well to the ways of her household, and eateth not the bread of idleness.

Her children arise up, and call her blessed; her husband also, and he praiseth her.

Favour is deceitful, and beauty is vain: but a woman that feareth the Lord, she shall be praised.

Give her of the fruit of her hands; and let her own works praise her in the gates.

Proverbs 31:10–31

My mother knew what it was like to be in the marketplace. In her younger days she had been a buyer at Marshall Field's in Chicago. Throughout all her life she was a professional artist. Yet she was always woman first and foremost, and she had the complete adoration of her husband. To me she fulfilled the image of the woman of Proverbs 31. She was:

> Gentle, yet not weak,
> Strong, yet not abrasive,
> Wise, yet not arrogant,
> Godly, yet not intolerant.

Particularly as I watched my parents grow older I realized more consciously the deep mutual love they had for each other. Maybe it was because I was older, too, and more perceptive. Each respected the other as being equal, yet my father was always the head of the home. They perceived it as a difference in role, not as a lessening of worth.

After my mother's death a few years ago, I was the only family member left to go through her things. It was a balmy Sunday afternoon when I came across a box of old letters. My father had written them from Seattle, in the last quarter of 1941, while he was away working in defense at the outset of World War II. My mother had apparently gotten them out after my father's death a few years earlier and had kept them hidden away to read for her comfort. They were ordinary letters about family, money for bills, plans to buy a house. They were newsworthy letters about war, climaxing with the bombing of Pearl Harbor. They were patriotic letters from a man who loved his country. Above all, they were love letters, and as such they were filled with all the little details of emotions and actions that make up the whole of the love relationship between a man and a woman.

As I read these letters from a lover to his beloved, my father to my mother, I realized with a start that when they were written my parents had been the same age as I was on that Sunday afternoon. Suddenly we were three adults, not just a grieving daughter and her parents. To use Madeleine L'Engle's idea, which I have referred to so often, I would never again be anyone's child. I became fully aware for the first time that from my mother as woman and from my father's treatment of her as woman I had learned at such an early age what it is to be God's woman in this century.

SOURCE NOTES

CHAPTER ONE

1. William Manchester, *American Caesar* (Boston: Little, Brown and Co., 1978), 272.
2. Ibid., 187.
3. Ibid., 653.
4. "She Was a Phantom of Delight," *An Oxford Anthology of English Poetry,* ed. Howard Foster Lowry and Willard Thorp, 2nd ed. (New York: Oxford University Press, 1956), 647.

CHAPTER TWO

1. Anne Bradstreet, "Some Verses Upon the Burning of Our House, July 10th, 1666," *American Heritage,* ed. Leon Howard, Louis B. Wright, and Carl Bode, vol. 1 (Boston: D. C. Heath and Co., 1955), 51.
2. Anne Bradstreet, "The Tenth Muse Lately Sprung Up in America, The Prologue," ibid., 48.
3. Ibid.

CHAPTER THREE

1. Ralph Waldo Emerson, "The American Scholar," *American Heritage,* ed. Leon Howard, Louis B. Wright,

and Carl Brode, vol. 1 (Boston: D. C. Heath and Co., 1955), 621.

2. Elizabeth Skoglund, *The Whole Christian* (New York: Harper and Row, 1976), 3–4.

3. Charles H. Spurgeon, "Discouragement," *His* (February, 1962), 8.

4. Sigmund Freud, quoted by Sackler et. al in "Recent Advances in Psychobiology and Their Impact on General Practice," *Inter. Record of Med.*, 170:1551 (1957).

5. Ronald V. Norris, with Colleen Sullivan, *PMS* (New York: Berkley Books, 1984), 155–56.

6. Ibid., 179.

7. Ibid.

8. Harvey M. Ross, "Megavitamins," *Journal of Orthomolecular Psychiatry*, 3, no. 4 (1974).

9. Viktor E. Frankl, *Man's Search for Meaning* (New York: Simon and Schuster, 1962), 106.

10. Frederick W. Faber, "Souls of Men, Why Will Ye Scatter," Paul Beckwith, ed., *Hymns* (Chicago: Inter-Varsity Press, 1959), 85.

11. Catherine Marshall, *Beyond Our Selves* (New York: Avon Books, 1968), 162–164.

12. A. B. Simpson, *Alliance Weekly*.

13. Charles H. Spurgeon, "Discouragement," *His* (February, 1962), 8.

CHAPTER FOUR

1. H. A. Ironside, *Addresses on the Song of Solomon* (New York: Loizeaux Brothers, 1933), 17–21.

2. J. Hudson Taylor, *Union and Communion* (Chicago: Moody Press), 111.

3. H. A. Ironside, *In the Heavenlies* (New York: Loizeaux Brothers, 1837), 278.

4. W. Robertson, ed., *The Expositor's Bible*, vol. 6 (Grand Rapids, Mich.: Eerdman's Publishing Co., 1947), 88.

5. Ibid., 89.

6. Adam Clarke, ed., *The New Testament of Our Lord and Saviour Jesus Christ*, vol. 1 (Nashville: Abingdon Press), 189.

7. Viktor E. Frankl, *The Doctor and the Soul* (New York: Vintage Books, 1973), 140.

8. Rollo May, *Love and Will* (New York: W. W. Norton & Co., 1969), 104.

CHAPTER FIVE

1. Elizabeth Skoglund, *Decision* (1967), 28–29.

2. Rollo May, *Love and Will* (New York: Dell Publishing Co., 1981), 115–116.

3. Colin M. Turnbull, *The Human Cycle* (New York: Simon and Schuster, 1983), 26.

4. Peter Singer and Deane Wells, *Making Babies* (New York: Charles Scribner's Sons, 1985), 176.

5. Ibid., 82.

6. May, *Love and Will*, 119.

7. Turnbull, *The Human Cycle*, 29.

8. Ibid., 33–34.

9. Ibid., 34.

10. Truman Capote, *A Christmas Memory* (New York: Random House, 1956), 77–78.

11. Ibid., 101, 102.

CHAPTER SIX

1. R. H. Charles, *The Teaching of the New Testament in Divorce* (London: Williams and Norgate, 1921), 91–111.

2. Guy Duty, *Divorce and Remarriage* (Minneapolis: Bethany Fellowship, 1967), 29.

3. Ibid., 40.

4. Ibid., 18.

5. Theodore Woolsey, *Essay on Divorce and Divorce Legislation* (New York: Scribner, 1869), 134–35.

6. J. B. Lightfoot, *Notes on the Epistles of St. Paul* (Grand Rapids, Mich.: Zondervan, 1895), 226.

7. Matthew Henry's Commentary, 1st. Cor. 7:15.

CHAPTER SEVEN

1. For further discussion on the concept of safety zones, please refer to Elizabeth Skoglund, *Safety Zones* (Waco, Tex.: Word Books, 1986).

2. Kati Morton, *Wallenberg* (New York: Random House, 1982), 135.

3. Ibid., 136.

4. P. D. James, *A Taste for Death* (New York: Alfred A. Knopf, 1986), 301–302.